Swedish

An Essential Grammar

2nd edition

This fully revised second edition of *Swedish: An Essential Grammar* incorporates a large number of changes of detail and examples throughout, all made with the aim of clarifying the explanations and updating the idioms and advice on current usage. The bibliography has been expanded and a number of tables clarified.

Swedish: An Essential Grammar provides a fresh and accessible description of the language. It is suitable for independent study or for class-based tuition. The explanations are free of jargon and emphasis has been placed on the areas of Swedish that pose a particular challenge for English-speaking learners.

Features include:

- Detailed contents list
- Many tables and diagrams for extra clarity
- Separate glossary of linguistic and grammatical terms
- Detailed index, with numerous key Swedish and English words

Philip Holmes was formerly Reader in Scandinavian Studies at the University of Hull and is now a freelance translator.

Ian Hinchliffe is a freelance translator, living in Sweden.

Routledge Essential Grammars

Essential Grammars are available for the following languages:

Arabic (forthcoming)
Chinese
Danish
Dutch
English
Finnish
German
Modern Greek
Modern Hebrew
Hindi (forthcoming)
Hungarian
Norwegian
Polish
Portuguese
Spanish
Swedish
Thai
Urdu

Other titles of related interest published by Routledge:

Colloquial Swedish
Swedish: A Comprehensive Grammar
Swedish Dictionary

Swedish

An Essential Grammar

2nd edition

 **Philip Holmes and Ian Hinchliffe**

 Routledge
Taylor & Francis Group

LONDON AND NEW YORK

First published 1997
by Routledge
2 Park Square, Milton Park, Abingdon, Oxon OX14 4RN

This edition first published 2008
by Routledge
2 Park Square, Milton Park, Abingdon, Oxon OX14 4RN

Simultaneously published in the USA and Canada
by Routledge
711 Third Avenue, New York, NY 10017, USA

Routledge is an imprint of the Taylor & Francis Group, an informa business

© 1997, 2008 Philip Holmes and Ian Hinchliffe

Typeset in Sabon and Gill by
Florence Production Ltd, Stoodleigh, Devon

British Library Cataloguing in Publication Data
A catalogue record for this book is available from the British Library

Library of Congress Cataloging in Publication Data
Holmes, Philip
 Swedish: an essential grammar/Philip Holmes and Ian Hinchliffe.
 – 2nd ed.
  p. cm. – (Routledge essential grammars)
 1. Swedish language – Grammar. I. Hinchliffe, Ian. II. Title.
 PD5112.H67 2009
 439.782'421 – dc22
 2007039675

ISBN10: 0–415–45800–5 (pbk)
ISBN10: 0–203–92893–8 (ebk)

ISBN13: 978–0–415–45800–9 (pbk)
ISBN13: 978–0–203–92893–6 (ebk)

Contents

Chapter 11   Conjunctions

Chapter 12   Word order and sentence structure

Chapter 13   Word formation   207

Chapter 14   Orthography   217

Chapter 15   Punctuation   220

Contents

Preface

In this book we hope to do two things: first, to provide learners of Swedish with a concise description of the structure of the language, as well as some account of spelling, punctuation, word formation and the differences between spoken and written Swedish; and second, to describe in greater detail those areas of Swedish that in our experience may pose a challenge for English-language learners.

The book is largely traditional in its approach and terminology. Most of the linguistic and grammatical terms used are explained in a separate glossary at the end of the book. There is also an index that should in many cases serve as a starting point for a search.

With its many tables and charts the book is intended to be easy to use; it will often be possible for the learner to predict patterns in many new words from just a few simple rules.

Translations of many of the examples are provided. These translations have been kept fairly literal in order to help the learner see contrasts and correlations between Swedish and English.

We would like to thank Olle Kjellin for his invaluable help in preparing the sections on pronunciation, stress and accent, and Claes Christian Elert for permission to use ideas and examples from his *Ljud och ord i svenskan 2* (Stockholm, 1981). Many other students and colleagues, including Brita Green, Jyrki Pietarinen and Vera Croghan, have provided valuable suggestions.

Learners who have progressed to an intermediate level or simply seek more thorough explanations of points of grammar and usage may wish to refer to our much more detailed *Swedish: A Comprehensive Grammar* (Routledge, second edition 2003).

Second edition

The first edition of this book came out in 1997, which preceded the publication of *Svenska Akademiens Grammatik* in 1999. This second edition involves a number of changes, not least a new categorization of noun declensions in Chapter 3 according to the new scheme proposed in *Svenska Akademiens Grammatik*.

There are also numerous changes of detail and examples throughout, all made with the aim of clarifying the explanations and updating the idioms and advice on current usage.

Symbols and abbreviations used in the text

[i:]	phonetic script. The phonetic symbols used are those of the International Phonetic Alphabet
r<u>o</u>lig	long stressed vowel, long consonant
r<u>o</u>ll	short stressed vowel
köp<u>a</u>	unstressed vowel
'kalla, stu'd<u>e</u>ra	stressed syllable
lite(t), (att)	letter, syllable or word may be omitted
ring**er**	stem **ring** plus ending -**er**
förr/förut	alternatives
hann (← hinna)	**hann** derives from **hinna**
x → **y**	**x** becomes **y**, e.g. when an ending is added
⊗	no ending is added, to distinguish a word or form from one to which an ending is added
*	irregular forms
adj.	adjective
adv.	adverb
C	consonant
CA	clausal adverbial
conj.	conjunction
cons.	consonant
FE	first element
FV	finite verb
IP	infinitive phrase
itr	intransitive
L	link
lit.	literally
MC	main clause
NFV	non-finite verb
NP	indefinite noun phrase
OA	other adverbial

Obj/comp, O/C	object/complement
Part	verb particle
prep.	preposition
S	subject
SC, subcl	subordinate clause
T	topic
tr.	transitive
V	vowel
V-question	question introduced by an interrogative pronoun (V-word)
W	words brought forward, as being more important
X^1, X^2	extra position

Introduction

0.1   Some advice for the beginner

In our opinion the secret to being able to speak and write Swedish well lies in three main areas – pronunciation, stress and word order – but an ability to manipulate the language also requires familiarity with several other basic areas of grammar.

Learning Swedish pronunciation is aided by the fact that Swedish is a phonetic language – that is to say, a particular group of letters nearly always corresponds to a particular sound (unlike English which is notorious for its lack of this correspondence, e.g. 'rough, through, bough, cough', etc.). It is possible to learn a few simple rules for Swedish pronunciation which are outlined at the beginning of this book, and which are accurate predictors in nearly all cases, the only exceptions being foreign loanwords.

Stress is important too, both as regards which words in the sentence have stress and where within a particular word the stress comes. This is explained in 2.1 f.

Swedish also has two word accents, which is why Swedes seem to 'sing' when they pronounce some words. The rules for the occurrence of these accents are detailed in 2.3 ff.

Word order and sentence structure are the basic building blocks of the language, a sure foundation that cannot be ignored if the learner wishes to speak and write understandable Swedish beyond a very basic level. Swedish main clause word order, for example, is much more flexible than English order: the sentence more often begins with a word (or words) other than the subject, and sentence elements may appear in several different positions in main and subordinate clauses. A large section of this book is devoted to a systematic account of word order.

Similarities between Swedish and English

This is a comparative grammar, deliberately concentrating on the differences between Swedish and English, some of which we have just outlined, and thereby addressing specifically the needs of English-speaking learners. But it is also necessary to bear in mind just how *similar* these two languages are. A few of the major similarities which will help the learner acquire a knowledge of Swedish are outlined below.

0.2.1 | *Vocabulary*

1 Both Swedish and English are Germanic languages and they possess a large core vocabulary of words that are identical or almost identical:

> **arm, fot, finger, gräs, hus, knä, lamm, oss, skarp, son, två, tre, vi**
> arm, foot, finger, grass, house, knee, lamb, us, sharp, son, two, three, we

2 Many English and American-English words have been borrowed into Swedish:

> **baby, bestseller, check, cykel, deodorant, jeans, jobb, match, potatis, reporter, service**

0.2.2 | *Grammar*

1 In both languages only nominative and genitive cases are found for nouns:

skepparen i båten	the skipper in the boat
skepparens katt	the skipper's cat

Both languages have subject and object forms of pronouns:

vi	we
oss	us

2 A similar distinction is found between adjectives and adverbs:

dyr	dear
dyrt	dearly

3 The languages have similar methods for comparing adjectives:

- with inflexional endings:

fet	fat
fetare	fatter
fetast	fattest

- without inflexional endings:

typisk	typical
mer typisk	more typical
mest typisk	most typical

4 Both languages have weak verbs with a dental ending (incorporating -d/-t) in the past tense:

Vi cyklade.	We cycled.
De kysste mig.	They kissed me.

5 Both languages have strong verbs with a vowel change in the past tense:

Vi sitter.	We sit.
Vi satt.	We sat.

6 The languages have similar modal auxiliary verbs:

kan, ska, måste	can, shall, must
De kan komma.	They can come.

7 The languages have a similar use of tenses:

Vi är här nu.	We are here now.
Han kom i april men han ska åka hem nästa vecka.	He came in April but he will go home next week.
Han har studerat i England.	He has studied in England.

3

8 The languages have a similar use of the formal subject (Sw. **det** = 'it/there'):

Det är kallt här.	It is cold here.
Det finns ett museum där.	There is a museum there.

9 Both languages have inverted (verb-subject) word order for questions:

Var är vi?	Where are we?
Är du sjuk?	Are you sick?

10 Both languages have only pre-positioned attributive adjectives:

en varm sommar	a warm summer
den varma sommaren	the warm summer

Chapter 1

Pronunciation

The phonetic script used here is that of the International Phonetic Association, and English equivalents are those of educated southern British English.

Vowels

The contrast between stressed and unstressed vowels is important in Swedish:

Stressed vowels may be either long or short:

   m<u>a</u>t   [mɑːt]   **m<u>att</u>**   [mat]

Unstressed vowels are always short:

   ställ<u>e</u>   [stɛlə]   **k<u>ö</u>p<u>e</u>r**   [çøːpər]

Short vowels are very short, shorter than in English. Long vowels are very long, longer than in English.

1.1.1 | *Stressed vowels and their pronunciation*

Nine different letters represent 21 different vowel sounds:

Back vowels

A		Å		O			
[ɑː]	[a]	[oː]	[ɔ]	[ɷː]	[ɷ]	[oː]	[ɔ]
glas	glass	hål	håll	rot	rott	ordna	kopp
dam	damm	gråt	grått	mor	moster	kol	boll
tak	tack	mås	måste	tro	trodde	son	folk

Front vowels

U		E					Ä		
[ʉ:]	[u]	[e:]	[ɛ]	[æ:]	[æ]	[ɛ:]	[ɛ]	[æ:]	[æ]
brun	brunn	fet	fett	Per	herr	väg	vägg	bära	märka
bus	buss	vek	veck	erfaren	verk	räka	räcka	kära	kärra
ful	full	heta	hetta	Erling	Sverige	släpa	släppa	järn	värk

I		Y		Ö			
[i:]	[i]	[y:]	[y]	[ø:]	[ø]	[œ:]	[œ]
fin	finns	byt	bytt	hög	högg	höra	förra
sil	sill	nys	nyss	mjöl	mjölk	gör	större
piga	pigga	flyta	flytta	blöta	blötta	för	först

Notes:

1 Pronunciation of letter O: When long the pronunciation [ɷ:] is more common than [o:], e.g. **stor** [stɷ:r] is more usual than **ordna** [o:ɖna]. When short the pronunciation [ɔ] is more common than [ɷ] e.g. **kosta** [kɔsta] is more usual than **ost** [ɷst].

2 In the pronunciation of some vowels, especially A, Å, O, U there is a marked difference in quality (position of tongue and lips) between long and short.

3 Pronunciation of E, Ä, Ö before R is more open than in other positions.

4 Some long vowels in Swedish are diphthongs ending in a fricative end-phase:

   i [iʲ] y [yʲ] u [uʷ] o [ɷʷ]

5 In the combination **eu** in loanwords U is pronounced as V (or F before T):

   neuros [nevro:s], **terapeut** [terapeft]

But notice also: **Europa** [erɷ:pa]

Approximate equivalent to pronunciation (Here 'English' = British English):

Long a   [ɑ:]   'a' in English 'father, dark'
Short a   [a]   'a' in English 'hat, hand'
Long å   [o:]   'a' in English 'all', but with lip-rounding
Short å   [ɔ]   'o' in English 'hot'
Long o   [ɷʷ]   'oo' in English 'doom, moon', with extreme lip-rounding and w-like fricative end-phase
Short o   [ɷ]   'oo' in English 'book' with less extreme lip-rounding
Long u   [ʉʷ]   Long **u** has no equivalent but is similar to 'u' in English 'futile', 'putrid'. With extreme lip-rounding and w-like fricative end-phase

6

Short u	[u]	'u' in English 'full', lax lip-rounding
Long e	[e:]	No equivalent in English, cf. French 'été'
Short e	[ɛ]	'e' in English 'pen', 'best'
Long ä	[ɛ:]	'ea' in English 'bear', but longer
Short ä	[e]	'e' in English 'pen', 'best'
Long i	[i:ʲ]	'ee' in English 'bee' but more closed and j-like fricative end-phase (i.e. like a Swedish j)
Short i	[i]	'i' in English 'hit', 'miss'
Long y	[y:ʲ]	No equivalent in English, cf. German 'ü' in 'Tür' Open lip-rounding with j-like fricative end phase (i.e. like a Swedish j)
Short y	[y]	No equivalent in English, cf. German 'ü' in 'dünn'
Long ö	[ø:]	No equivalent in English, cf. French 'eu' in 'peu' but much longer with lip-rounding
Short ö	[ø]	'u' in English 'hurt', though much shorter
NB i/y		The only difference is that y has lip-rounding
y/u		The difference is the quality of the fricative end-phase

1.1.2 | Pronunciation of unstressed vowels

Unstressed vowels (marked ̥) occur in unstressed syllables before or after a stressed syllable:

för'stḁ̊   po̥'ta̱tis   'skri̱ve̥r   'pojke̥

1 Unstressed **i** in suffixes -ig, -lig, -isk, -ing, -is, -it:

sa̱ndi̱g, böjli̱g, ty̱pi̱sk, parke̱ri̱ng, go̱di̱s, sprungi̱t

2 Unstressed **a** in many inflexional endings and suffixes:

bi̱la̱r (noun plural)	**bi̱la̱rna** (noun plural definite)
då̱liga̱ (adjective plural)	**ro̱liga̱st** (adjective superlative)
ta̱la̱ (verb infinitive)	**ta̱la̱r** (verb present)
ta̱la̱de (verb past)	**ta̱la̱t** (verb supine)
a̱rbeta̱re (noun denoting person, occupation)	
he̱mma̱, bo̱rta̱ (adverbs of location)	

3 Unstressed o

flickor (noun plural) Sometimes pronounced [flikər], [flikor] or [flikɷr]

nio, tio (numerals) Often pronounced [niːə], [tiːə]

tjugo (numeral) Pronounced [çʉːgu] or [çʉːgə]

Before **r** [ɷ] alternates with [o]: **motor** [mɷːtɷr] or [mɷːtɔr]

4 Unstressed e

Usually [ə]: **gubbe, pojke, cykel, vacker, damer, köper, skriven**

Notice that e is never silent; cf.

| English 'spade' [speid] | Swedish **spade** | [spɑːdə] |
| English 'rune' [ruːn] | Swedish **Rune** | [rʉːnə] |

1.1.3 Vowel length

1 Rules for predicting vowel length from written form: (V = Vowel, C = Consonant)

Rule 1	Stressed vowels in open syllables (ending in a vowel) are long:	**få**	V
Rule 2	Stressed vowels followed by one consonant are long	**får**	VC
Rule 3	Stressed vowels followed by two or more consonants are short:	**fått**	VCC
	(long consonant or consonant group)	**fångna**	VCC
		fångst	VCCCC
Rule 4	Unstressed vowels are always short:	**tala, köper**	

In accordance with Rule 1:
Stressed vowels before other vowels are long: **trio, Dorotea**

In accordance with Rule 3:
Stressed vowels before -**sj**, -**ng** (and their equivalents) are short as these consonant groups each represent one consonant sound – [ʃ] and [ŋ] – respectively: **usch, lång, restaurang**

Stressed vowels before **-rm, -rb** are short (cf. English): **arm, charm, arbete**

An exception to Rule 2:
Stressed vowels before **-x** [ks] are short as **-x** represents
two consonant sounds [ks]: **sax, flaxa, maximum**

An exception to Rule 3:
Stressed vowels before **-rn, -ln, -rl, -rd** are long, as
these consonant groups each represent one consonant
sound, [ɳ], [ɳ], [ɭ] and [ɖ] respectively: **b<u>a</u>rn, <u>a</u>ln, h<u>ä</u>rlig, g<u>å</u>rd**

2 Vowel length and inflexional endings

Despite Rule 3 above, vowel length is not normally affected by the addition
of inflexional endings or word formation suffixes:

f<u>i</u>n   **f<u>i</u>nt** (neuter ending on adjective)

s<u>ö</u>ka   **s<u>ö</u>kte** (past tense ending on verb)

sj<u>u</u>k   **sj<u>u</u>klig** (adjectival suffix)

However, if the stem ends in, or the inflexional ending begins in, a **d/t**,
then the vowel is shortened according to Rule 3:

bet<u>y</u>da   **bet<u>y</u>dde** (past tense ending on verb)

m<u>ö</u>ta   **m<u>ö</u>tte** (past tense ending on verb)

v<u>i</u>t   **v<u>i</u>tt** (neuter ending on adjective)

Similarly, if the stem ends in a long stressed vowel and the inflexional ending
begins in a **d/t**, then the vowel is shortened according to Rule 3:

bl<u>å</u>   **bl<u>å</u>tt** (neuter ending on adjective)

kl<u>ä</u>   **kl<u>ä</u>dd** (past participle ending on verb)

tr<u>e</u>   **tr<u>e</u>ttio** ('-ty' ending on numeral)

sj<u>u</u>   **sj<u>u</u>tton** ('-teen' ending on numeral)

1.1.4	*Syllable length*

1 A syllable consists of a vowel on its own or accompanied by one or more consonants before or after the vowel. There are the same number of syllables in a word as there are vowels. The following are all syllables:

ö	på	två	att	alm	halm	hos	hemskt
V	CV	CCV	VCC	VCC	CVCC	CVC	CVCCCC

Many words have two syllables:

poj-ke	å-ker	kal-la
CVC-CV	V-CVC	CVC-CV

Some words have many syllables:

parkera:			industriarbetare:						
par	-ke	-ra	in	-du	-stri	-ar	-be	-ta	-re
CVC	-CV	-CV	VC	-CV	-CCCV	-VC	-CV	-CV	-CV

2 All stressed syllables in Swedish are long, and contain:

EITHER a long vowel and single
consonant: a̱l   i̱s

Or

a short vowel + a long consonant: a̱ll   a̱lm   a̱rm   a̱rg
(double consonant or consonant   a̱ll-tid a̱l-mar a̱r-mar a̱r-ga
group)   hi̱ss   li̱s-ta

See also 1.1.1 f above.

1.2   Consonants and consonant groups

There are 20 different letters representing 23 different sounds.

Consonants **b, d, f, g, l, m, n, p, r, s, t, z** may be doubled:

mamma, falla, hatt, jazz

When they either precede or follow a vowel, the letters **b, d, f, h, m, n, v** are usually pronounced as in English. But notice also the pronunciation of **d** in the group **rd** in 1.2.6 below.

Consonants **p**, **t** and **k** are usually pronounced [p], [t], [k] (but see also 1.2.4 below), though they may also be strongly aspirated (with an exhalation of breath):

pappa [pʰapa] **ta** [tʰaː] **kasta** [kʰasta]

Remember: Vowels are short before a long consonant (double consonant or consonant group):

h<u>a</u>l – h<u>a</u>ll

1.2.1	*s, z, c, sc*

s [s] Swedish s is like 's' in English 'sit', *not* as z in English 'please':

Lisa, läsa, stycke, ros, musik, stum

z [s] is pronounced exactly as Swedish s:

zon, zoologi

Exception
[ts] in some German names: **Schweiz**

c [s] as in English 'centre' before **e, i, y**:

centrum, cirka, cykel

[k] as in English 'cotton' before **a, o, u**:

camping, cocktail, curry

sc [s] as in English 'scene':

scen, fosforescent

[ʃ] as in English 'fascist':

fascist, crescendo, fascinerande

1.2.2 *j, gj, dj, hj, lj*

j [j] is pronounced as consonant 'y' in English 'young' before all vowels and at the end of a word:

**ja, jul, jobb, jeans, Jimmy, Jenny, järn
haj, hej, detalj, familj, kampanj**

[ʃ] in a few loanwords:

à jour, journal, journalist, jalusi, projekt

[j] gj-, dj-, hj-, lj- the first letter is silent and these groups are pronounced as Swedish j. Notice therefore that the following pairs are pronounced in the same way:

gjord – jord   djärv – järv   hjul – jul   ljus – jus

1.2.3 *r, t, l, x, w*

r [r] in Central and Northern Sweden is a tongue-tip trilled 'r' as in Scottish. This sound is found at the beginning and end of syllables:

rum, dörr, norr

[ɹ] in Southern Sweden there is a tongue root 'r', not unlike German and French 'r'.

t [t] is pronounced with the tip of the tongue on the back of the upper teeth and is thus slightly 'sharper' than in English:

titta, tratt

Note: In some loanwords t may be pronounced as [ʃ] in words in **-tion: station** [staʃɷ:n], **motion** [mɷʃɷ:n]; and in **-ti: initiativ** [iniʃi:ati:v], **aktie** [akʃi:ə].

l [l] is pronounced as 'l' in English 'like', *not* as in 'elk':

lilla, till, Ulla

x [ks] is voiceless and pronounced as 'x' in English 'excited' *not* as in 'exist':

växa, exempel, strax

Note: In loanwords x in an initial position is pronounced as s: **xenofobi.**

w [v] is pronounced as 'v' and is nowadays found only in names and loanwords:

Wasa, whisky, wellpapp, WC [ve:se:]

1.2.4 *g, k, sk*

The pronunciation of initial **g-**, **k-**, **sk-** varies according to the vowel following:

1 'Soft' g-, k-, sk-

Before the vowels **e, i, y, ä, ö** these consonants are palatalized:

g- [j]   is pronounced as Swedish **j** or English consonant 'y' in 'young':

> **Gösta, gymnasium, gärna**

k- [ç]   is pronounced something like German 'ch' in 'ich':

> **köpa, källare, kyrka**

sk- [ʃ]   is pronounced something like 'sh' in English 'shirt', but further back and always with lip-rounding:

> **skinka, skön, skära**

Like soft **g** [j], syllables ending in **-lg** [lj], **-rg** [rj]:

> **helg**, **älg**, **Borg**, **Berg**

Note also: **galge**, **Norge**, **Sverige** [sværjə], **orgel**

Like soft **k** [ç], words beginning with the letters **kj-**, **tj-**, **ch-**:

> **kjol, kjortel, tjugo, check**

(This occurs before all vowels, cf. **k-**)

2 'Sje-ljud' (soft **sk** sound or **sj** sound)

There are two variants of the Swedish sound:

[ʃ] 'Back **sj**-sound', formed by raising the back of the tongue:

> **skina, skytte**

[ʂ] 'Front **sj**-sound', formed by raising the middle or front of the tongue:

> **sköterska, Askim** (Pronunciation varies in dialect and idiolect.)

Like back **sj**, words beginning with the letters **sj-, skj-, stj-**, and some loans with **ch-, sch-**:

> **sju, skjorta, stjärna, choklad, schack**

Like front **sj**, most words ending in **-sion**, **-tion**, **-rs**, **-sch** and their derivatives:

vision, station, kors, Anders, dusch, missionera

Note:
Some loanwords in **g**, **j** may be pronounced with either front **sj** or back **sj**:

generell, religiös, energi, journalist

3 'Hard' **g-**, **k-**, **sk-**

Before the vowels **o, u, a, å** these are pronounced as in English:

g- [g] is pronounced as 'g' in English 'gate':

gata, gå, god

k- [k] is pronounced as 'k' in English 'keep':

kaka, kål, kul

sk- [sk] is pronounced as 'sk' in English 'skill':

ska, skor, skugga

They are also usually 'hard' after all vowels:

Stig, lägga, Sveg   **Erik, doktor, lök**   **ask, besk, diska**

Exceptions to the rules found for pronunciation given in (1)–(3) above are found in the following words (mostly loans):

k	[k]	before a soft vowel	**arkiv, kille, fakir, monarki, Kiruna, bukett, keps, kö, prekär**
sk	[sk]	before a soft vowel	**skippa, skiss, skepsis, sketch, skelett**
sk	[ʃ]	before a hard vowel	**människa, marskalk**

1.2.5 *ng, gn, kn, mn*

-ng [ŋ] is pronounced as one sound, as in southern English 'singer':

Inga, pengar, gånger

-gn [ŋn] is pronounced as Swedish **ng** + **n**, as in English 'ring-necked':

vagn, Ragnar, regn

gn- [gn] unlike English 'gnaw' the g is pronounced , as in English 'pregnant':

gnaga, Gnosjö

kn- [kn] unlike English 'knife' the k is pronounced, as in 'locknut':

kniv, knä, Knut

-mn [mn] unlike English 'autumn' the n is pronounced, as in 'remnant':

hamn, namn

1.2.6 | *rs, rd, rt, rn, rl*

In Central and Northern Swedish these groups produce 'alveolar retroflex' sounds:

rs [ʂ] **rd** [ɖ] **rt** [ʈ] **rn** [ɳ] **rl** [ɭ]

These are so called because the tongue tip is bent backwards against the alveolar ridge behind the upper teeth rather than (in the case of **d, t, n, l** alone) behind the teeth themselves. In the case of **rd, rt, rn, rl** these sounds may be difficult for the non-Swede to distinguish from normal **d, t, n, l**:

bord	**bort**	**barn**	**Karl**
bod	**bot**	**ban**	**kal**

But **rs** [ʂ] is much easier to hear. It is the 'front sj-sound', pronounced as 'sh' in English 'sheep':

fors, Lars, varsågod, störst, mars, person

See also 1.2.11.

1.2.7 | *Omitting -d, -g, -t, -k, -l*

1 The final **-g** of adjectives ending in **-ig** or **-lig** is nearly always omitted in the spoken language:

färdig, rolig	[fɛːɖi], [rʊːli]
färdigt, roligt	[fɛːɖit], [rʊːlit]
färdiga, roliga	[fɛːɖia], [rʊːlia]

15

2 In many commonly used words a final -d, -g or -t is often dropped in pronunciation. The final -d, -g or -t of many common monosyllabic nouns is unpronounced even in the plural and definite forms of the noun.

god, goda	[gɷ:], [gɷ:a]
röd, röda	[rø:], [rø:a]
med	[me:]
ved	[vɛ]
vid	[vi]
vad	[va]
det	[de:]
mycket, litet	[mykə], [li:tə]
alltid, aldrig	[alti], [aldri]
något, inget	[nɔt], [iŋə]
måndag, tisdag . . .	[mɔnda], [tista] (NB short unstressed a)
bröd, brödet, bröden	[brø:], [brø:t], [brø:n]
träd, trädet, träden	[trɛ:], [trɛ:t], [trɛ:n]
jag	[jɑ:]
dag, dagen, dagar	[dɑ:], [dɑ:n], [dɑ:r] (NB long a)

Notes:

1 The -t ending in the supine form of some first conjugation verbs is frequently omitted in spoken Swedish.

2 For the pronunciation of pronominal forms **mig, dig, sig, det, de, dem**, see 1.2.10.

3 The spoken forms of **huvud**, 'head', an irregular 5th declension noun, are:

sg. [huve] **huvud** pl. [huven] **huvuden**
def.sg. [huvet] **huvudet** def.pl. [huvena] **huvudena**

4 The final -t is omitted in some French loanwords in spoken Swedish:

konsert, 'concert' is pronounced [kɔnser]; **kuvert**, 'envelope' is pronounced [kuver]

5 In some instances the -d, -g omitted is not at the end of the word. Some omissions are so common that the spoken form has become frequent even in the written language (see (b) below).

(a) Omitted in pronunciation but not in spelling:

bredvid	[brɛviːd] or [brɛvi] or [brɛːvɛ]
morgon	[mɔrɔn]
midsommar	[misɔmar]
förkläde, förklädet	[førklɛː], [førklɛːt]
trädgård, trädgården	[trɛːgoːd], [trɛːgoːɳ]

Notes:

1 Sometimes a truncated form of a noun ending in **-ad, -ag** may be used, but only in the definite singular form:

stad, staden	[stɑːd], [stɑn]
månad, månaden	[moːnad], [moːnan]
skillnad, skillnaden	[ʃilnad], [ʃilnan]
da(g), dagen	[dɑː], [dɑːn] NB. Indefinite singular form

2 Note the change of vowel length in expressions ending in -s such as:

i måndags	[i mɔndas] (short final vowel)
i tisdags	[i tiːstas] (short final vowel)

3 **-d-** between **r** and **s** is often not pronounced in spoken Swedish:

vårdslös	[voːʃløːs]

(b) Omitted in pronunciation and sometimes in spelling:

In many instances where **-d** + vowel or **-g** + vowel is omitted in spoken Swedish such omissions have become frequent in casual written Swedish.

Some common examples of this phenomenon follow. Note how the preceding vowel is shortened.

	någon, något (nån, nåt)	[nɔn], [nɔt] (short vowel)
(But:	**några)**	[noːra] (long vowel!)
	sådan sådant sådana	[sɔn], [sɔnt], [sɔna] (short vowel)
	(sån, sånt, såna)	
	sedan (sen)	[sɛn]
	någonsin, någonstans	[nɔnsin], [nɔnstans] (short vowel)
	(nånsin, nånstans)	

The omission of -d + vowel has been accepted in the singular indefinite form of three very common nouns and a number of less common ones:

fader pronounced and often written **far** [fɑːr]
(But: definite form **fadern** in written and spoken Swedish!)

moder pronounced and often written **mor** [moːr]
(But: definite form **modern** in written and spoken Swedish!)

broder pronounced and often written **bror** [broːr]
(But: definite form **brodern** in written and spoken Swedish!)

Note: farbrorn, farmorn are sometimes encountered in written Swedish.
Cf. also **ladugård**   pronounced [lɑːɡoːɖ].

Third conjugation verbs with stems in long **e** or long **ä** sounds followed by **-d** frequently omit the **-d** in the present tense (see 7.2.5):

(kläda) – kläder   pronounced and written **klär** [klɛːr]

(breda) – breder   pronounced and written **brer** [brɛːr]

(c) Omitted in pronunciation and usually omitted in spelling:

Several words with original forms containing **-d, -g** have now dropped these unpronounced letters even in written Swedish:

aderton   is now pronounced and spelt **arton** [ɑːʈɔn]

badstuga   is now pronounced and spelt **bastu**

förstuga   is now pronounced and spelt **farstu** [faʃtʉ]

Södermanland   is now pronounced and spelt **Sörmland**

The longer forms of these words are seen only rarely or in formal written Swedish.

4 The final syllable **-de** in the past tense of first conjugation verbs is usually dropped in spoken Swedish, such verbs thus ending in a short **-a** vowel sound.

han kallade   is pronounced [han kala]

vi ropade   is pronounced [viː roːpa]

Note: The final -de ending in the past tense of the verbs **lägga** and **säga** is usually omitted in spoken Swedish. The shorter forms thus created are **la** and **sa** (both with long vowel sounds). **Sa** is now the normal written form. (See 7.2.4.)

5 The final -t is often omitted in the spoken form of the first conjugation supine:

Vi har jobbat.   is pronounced [viː haː jɔba]

6 The -k of adjectives whose basic form ends in -k is not usually pronounced when followed by -t:

hemskt, kritiskt   [hɛmst], [kriːtist]

7 In a few well-defined words -l or -ll in spoken Swedish is generally omitted:

värld (and compounds)   [vɛːɖ]

karl, karln, karlar, chap   [kɑːr], [kɑːɳ], [kɑːrar]

(BUT: **Karl** as a boy's name   [kɑːɭ])

till   [ti]

skall in older written Swedish   [ska] now usually written **ska**

1.2.8	*Omitting -e*

The -e of the non-neuter definite (end) article -en is often omitted in spoken Swedish after -r or -l:

konduktören   [kɔnduktøːŋ]

salen   [sɑːln]

dörren   [dørŋ]

kvällen   [kvɛln]

The final unstressed -e of many non-neuter nouns ending in -**are,** which signify a trade or profession, is dropped in spoken Swedish before the definite singular (end) article -**n**:

bagaren, läraren, verkmästaren, become: **bagarn,** [bɑːgaɳ]
lärarn [lɛːraɳ], **verkmästarn** [værkmɛstaɳ] etc.

Note: The final -e in such words is usually dropped in both written and spoken Swedish when the words are used as a title before a name: **bagar Olsson, verkmästar Törnquist,** etc.

1.2.9 *Voiced consonants pronounced unvoiced before -s, -t*

The final voiced consonants -d, -g, -v of some common monosyllabic words are retained in written Swedish but become unvoiced -t, -k, -f in spoken Swedish when suffixed with -s. Note also that the preceding vowel is shortened before the suffixed -s.

hur dags, what time?	[hʉdaks]
i Guds namn, in Heaven's name	[i Guts namn]
till havs, at sea	[ti hafs]
högst, at most	[høkst]

Note: For **i måndags, i tisdags** etc., see 1.2.7 3(a) Note 2.

A voiced -g (or -gg) is pronounced unvoiced as -k before a suffixed -t:

styggt, wicked	[stykt]
sagt, said	[sakt]
lagt, laid	[lakt]
högt, high	[høkt] NB short vowel

A voiced -b (or -bb) is pronounced unvoiced as -p before a suffixed -s or -t:

Obs!, Note	[ɔps]
snabbt, quickly	[snapt]

A similar phenomenon occurs in compound words when an element of the compound ending in -d, -g, -v is followed by -s. The voiced consonant becomes unvoiced and the preceding vowel is frequently shortened:

dödstrött, dog tired	[døtstrøt]
stadsbo, town-dweller	[statsbɷ]
dagstidning, daily newspaper	[daksti:dniŋ]
skogsbryn, edge of the forest	[skɷksbry:n]
havsbad, beach	[hafsbɑ:d]

Notes:

1 The addition of a genitive -s does not normally affect vowel length. Compare:
   en dags vandring [dɑ:gs] and **en dagstur** [dakstʉ:r].

2 In the following cases complete assimilation of **t** to **s** has taken place:

matsäck	[masɛk]
statsråd	[stasroːd]
skjuts	[ʃus]

<h2>1.2.10   Written and spoken forms of some common words</h2>

1 Many of the Swedish personal pronouns are pronounced in a way that is not in accord with the standard written form.

jag	pronounced [jɑ]	**mig**	pronounced [mɛj]
du	(cf. note 1)	**dig**	pronounced [dɛj]
		honom	(cf. note 2)
		henne	(cf. note 2)
		sig	pronounced [sɛj]

2 **Mej, dej, sej** are now accepted in some informal writing as alternatives to **mig, dig, sig** (see 5.1).

Notes:

1 In very colloquial Swedish the **d-** of **du, dig** is frequently omitted following a verbal **-r** ending:

    Ser 'u nåt? (Ser du något?)   Can you see anything?

2 In the past **honom** and **henne** had spoken forms, but except in certain dialects, these are no longer common:

    honom was pronounced **'en** or **'n** after a vowel **Jag har aldrig sett 'en.**
    henne was pronounced **'na**   **Jag gav 'na pengarna.**

3 **Dom** for both subject (**de**) and object (**dem**) form is accepted in some informal writing. **Dom** is sometimes also seen in expressions like **dom här** and as the front article in, for example **dom nya bilarna**, in written Swedish, though this is regarded as slovenly.

4 **Det** is pronounced [de] (short vowel) when used as a pronoun and in expressions such as [de hɛː hʉːsət] (written **det här huset**) and [de nyːa hʉːsət] (written **det nya huset**). In the past **den, det** used as object had the spoken forms **'en** (**'n** after a vowel) and **'et** (**'t** after vowel) but, except in certain dialects, these are no longer common.

    Här har du geväret. Ta 't.   Here's your rifle. Take it!

5 In spoken Swedish the possessive pronouns for 1st and 2nd persons plural **vår**, **er** have colloquial forms which exist alongside the standard written forms:

Det är våran skola.	It's our school.
Är det eran skola?	Is it your school?
Det är vårat hus.	It's our house.
Är det erat hus?	Is it your house?

6 In addition to the examples in 1.2.7 ff there are other cases in which common written Swedish words are pronounced in a way that might not be expected:

Written Swedish	*Spoken Swedish*
förstås	[føʃtɔs]
och (unstressed position)	[ɔ]
och (stressed position)	[ɔk]
att, to (before infinitive)	[ɔ]
säga, säger, sa(de), sagt	[sɛːja] [sɛːjər] [sɑː] [sakt]
lade, lagt	[lɑː] [lakt]
stod	[stɷːg]
förstod	[føʃtːɷg]
vara, är, var, varit	[vɑː] (long vowel) [ɛː] [vɑː] [va]
ett ögonblick	[ɛt øːgɔmblik]

1.2.11 Assimilation

Where the final sound of one word and the initial sound of the next are difficult to pronounce together, some form of assimilation usually takes place in Swedish.

In fluent spoken Swedish **-r** as the last sound in a word before a word beginning with **s-** is assimilated with the **s-** to an **sj-** sound (see 1.2.6 above):

Hur sa?	is pronounced [hʉʃa]
Tack för senast	is pronounced [takføʃeːnast]
för stor	is pronounced [føʃtɷːr]

Note: This kind of assimilation is less common in southern Sweden than in the rest of the country.

In fluent spoken Swedish, assimilation of **r** occurs with a following **d, t, n, l** (see 1.2.10(2), Note 1 above):

Kommer du?	is pronounced [kɔmədu]

In fluent spoken Swedish, a final **-n** after a short vowel in a word which is not heavily stressed is pronounced **-m** before a following **b-**:

min bror, en boll   become   [mimbrɷːr], [ɛmbɔll]

Chapter 2

Stress and accent

The music of Swedish (prosody) is produced by three features:

Sentence stress	Which words in the sentence receive stress?
Word stress	Which parts of the word are stressed?
Accent	Which tone, single peak (Accent 1) or double peak (Accent 2), does the word possess?

2.1 Sentence stress

In principle all the semantically significant words in the sentence are stressed. In practice this may vary somewhat. In this paragraph different sentence elements (see 12.1 ff) are listed and the stress shown for different circumstances.

KEY: e = long stressed vowel, ẹ = short stressed vowel
e̥ = unstressed vowel

Rules	Examples
Subject	
Nouns are stressed	**Anna har köpt ett hus.** Anna has bought a house.
	Huset ligger vackert. The house is beautifully situated.
Pronouns are unstressed	**Det kostade mycket pengar.** It cost a lot of money
	Hon hade inte råd. She could not afford it.

23

Object

Nouns are stressed	**Hon äter middag.** She eats dinner. **Kalle möter Anna.** Kalle meets Anna.
Pronouns are unstressed	**Han möter henne.** **Han gör det.** He meets her. He does it.
Object pronouns beginning the sentence are stressed	**Honom har hon inte sett på länge.** She has not seen him for a long time.
For contrast, objects are stressed	**Jag tycker inte om honom, men jag gillar henne.** I do not like him, but I like her.

Verb

No object, then verb stressed	**Eva äter och dricker.** Eva is eating and drinking.
Object, then verb unstressed	**Eva dricker kaffe.** **Hon dricker inte te.** Eva drinks coffee. She does not drink tea.
Complement, then verb unstressed	**Hon blev polis.** She became a police officer. **Han är sjuk.** He is ill.
Formal subject, then verb unstressed	**Det ligger en bok på bordet.** There is a book lying on the table.
Auxiliary verbs are unstressed	**Hon ska dricka.** She is going to drink. **Jag måste gå nu.** I must go now.

Notice also:

For contrast, verbs are stressed	**Han målar inte väggarna utan tapetserar dem.** He does not paint the walls but wallpapers them.

Particle verbs: the particles are stressed, the verbs unstressed	**Han satte på sig hatten.** He put on his hat.	
	Föraren körde om bilen. The driver overtook the car.	
Adverbial		
Inte is unstressed	**Hon vill inte. De är inte hemma.** She does not want to. They are not at home.	
Other adverbials are usually stressed whether first or last in the sentence	**Här är han nu. Därför vill vi inte vänta längre.** Here he is now. That is why we do not want to wait any longer.	
	Stänger den inte tidigt idag? Doesn't it close early today?	

2.2 Word stress

Word stress is found only in words that have sentence stress.

1 Non-compounds:

Of these words, some 35 per cent are monosyllables, 40 per cent have initial stress on the first syllable and 25 per cent non-initial stress on a different syllable:

Words with initial stress:

'nyckel key	**'vinter** winter	**'köper** buys
'hallon raspberry	**'gata** street	

Words with non-initial stress:
words with the prefixes **be-, för-**:

be'strida contest	**be'tala** pay	**för'sök** attempt

words with the suffix **-era**:

par'k̲e̲ra	**ser'v̲e̲ra**
park	serve

many foreign loans:

restau'ra̲ng	**re'v̲y̲**	**inka'pa̲bel**
restaurant	review	incapable
etymo'lo̲g̲	**re'gi̲ster**	
etymologist	register	

words with foreign suffixes:

regi'ssö̲r̲	**gym'na̲st**	**musi'ka̲nt**
director	gymnast	musician

2 Compounds:

Compound words have a stress on each of the parts of the compound, but the melody of each part is different. This also varies from region to region.

In central Swedish: the first stress has a falling pitch ↘
the last stress has a rising pitch ↗

↘ ↗
hu̲snyckel
house key

↘ ↗
centra̲llasare̲tt
central hospital

↘ ↗
jä̲rnvägsrä̲ls
railway track

↘ ↗
la̲stbilsfö̲rare
truck driver

↘ ↗
S̲ J̲ (Sta̲tens järnvä̲gar)
State Railways

↘ ↗
S̲K̲F̲ (Sve̲nska ku̲llagerfabri̲ken)
Swedish Ball Bearing Company

2.3 Accent

There are two distinct accents (tones) for Swedish words of two or more syllables with sentence stress (and therefore also word stress). Compare the words **skriver** and **gammal**:

skri̲-ver	**ga̲m-mal**	Both have stress on the first syllable,
writes	old	but the balance of the stress differs:

```
4   1      3    2
skri-ver   gam-mal      They also have different tone
  ↗        ↘    ↗        patterns or melodies.
skriver   gammal
```

Gammal has accent 2 (tonal accent) with two tone peaks, falling-rising in central Swedish. (Notice that the second peak in accent 2 is identical with accent 1.)

Skriver has accent 1 with one tone peak (rising), the same as in stressed monosyllabic words:

```
   ↗           ↗            ↗
en bil      en buss      en man
a car       a bus        a man
```

2.4 Functions of accent 1/accent 2

Accent 2 is only found in polysyllabic words. The main function of accent 2 is to show that two syllables belong together – it has a 'connective function':

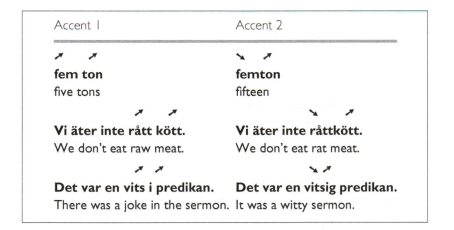

Accent 1	Accent 2
↗ ↗	↘ ↗
fem ton	**femton**
five tons	fifteen
↗ ↗	↘ ↗
Vi äter inte rått kött.	**Vi äter inte råttkött.**
We don't eat raw meat.	We don't eat rat meat.
↗ ↗	↘ ↗
Det var en vits i predikan.	**Det var en vitsig predikan.**
There was a joke in the sermon.	It was a witty sermon.

Accent 2 can also have a 'distinctive function': there are about 350 homophones which are distinguished only by their accents. Many of these minimal pairs are inflected forms of originally monosyllabic (accent 1) and originally bisyllabic (accent 2) words:

Accent I	Accent 2	
↗	↘ ↗	
and-en	**ande-n**	
(← **and** I syllable)		(← **ande** 2 syllables)
the duck	the spirit	
↗	↘ ↗	
brunn-en	**brunnen**	
(← **brunn** I syllable)		(← **brinna** 2 syllables)
the well	burned	
↗	↘ ↗	
Polen	**påle**	(← **pale** 2 syllables)
Poland	the pole	
↗	↘ ↗	
komma	**komma**	
comma	come	

2.5 Rules for accent 2

Accent I is found	Accent 2 is found
I In all *monosyllabic* words:	I In most *compounds*:
↗ ↗ ↗ ↗	↘ ↗ ↘↗ ↘ ↗
bok bil kallt först	**järnväg lastbil bokhylla**
book car cold first	railway truck bookshelf
	↘ ↗
	sjukhus
	hospital
2 In some *bisyllabic* words detailed below	2 In most other *polysyllabic words* with stress on the first syllable:
	↘↗ ↘ ↗ ↘↗ ↘ ↗
	flicka pojke sexton börjar
	girl boy sixteen begins
	↘↗ ↘ ↗ ↘ ↗ ↘↗ ↘ ↗
	bilar katterna pratat skrivet lättast
	cars the cats spoken written easiest

A The following features 'block'   Exceptions to this blocking
accent 2 (i.e. with accent 1)   (i.e. with accent 2)

(i) Endings in a *vowel* + **l**:

Nouns:

↗	↗	↗	↗	↘↗
cykel	**segel**	**fågel**	**medel**	**nyckel**
cycle	sail	bird	means	key

Adjectives:

↗	↗	
enkel	**simpel**	–
easy	simple	

(ii) Endings in a *vowel* + **n**:

Nouns:

↗	↗	↗	↗	↘↗	↘↗
öken	**socken**	**tecken**	**vatten**	**fruktan**	**tävlan**
desert	parish	sign	water	fear	competition

Adjectives:

	↘↗	↘↗	↘↗	↘↗
–	**egen**	**ledsen**	**öppen**	**skriven**
	own	sad	open	written

(and other Conjugation 4 participles)

(iii) Endings in a *vowel* + **r**:

Nouns:

↗	↗	↗	↗	↘↗	↘↗	↘↗
vinter	**teater**	**nummer**	**fönster**	**moder**	**syster**	**sommar**
winter	theatre	number	window	mother	sister	summer

Plurals with *mutation* + **er**:   Plurals *without mutation*:

↗	↗	↗		↘↗	↘↗	↘↗
böcker	**fötter**	**händer**	(cf. **flickor**	**stolar**	**katter**)
books	feet	hands		girls	chairs	cats

↗	↗
nätter	**städer**
nights	cities

Adjectives:

↗　　↗　　↗
vacker　mager　läcker　　　–
pretty　thin　delicious

Verbs in **-er** (present tense):　　*Verbs in* **-ar** (present tense)

↗　　　↗　　↗　　　↗　　　↘↗　↘↗　　↘↗　　↘↗
ringer　läser skriver äter　　**tittar målar badar lagar**
rings　reads writes eats　　looks paints bathes mends

(iv) Adjective comparative endings in **-re**, superlative endings in
-erst:

↗　　　↗　　　↗　　↗　　　　↘↗　　　↘↗
längre yngre　lägre större　(cf.　**lättare　lättast**)
longer younger lower bigger　　　easier　easiest

↗　　　　↗
överst　　ytterst
uppermost　outermost

(v) Adjective endings in **-isk, -sk**:

↗　　　↗　　　↗
typisk komisk engelsk
typical comical　English

(vi) Nouns ending in **-is, -iker**:

↗　　　↗　　　↗　　↗
dagis　kompis godis　lekis
nursery friend　　sweets nursery school

↗　　　↗
musiker tekniker
musician technician

(vii) Verbs with unstressed initial syllables:

↗　　　　↗
betalar　　förstår
pays　　　understands

(vii) Verbs ending in **-era**:

↗　　　　　↗　　　　　↗
fotograferar　　studerar　　socialiserar
takes photographs　studies　　socialises

B All nouns with end articles have the same accent as in the form
without end article

↗ ↗
en bil bilen
a car   the car

↘↗   ↘↗
en klocka klockan
a clock   the clock

↗ ↗
en kompis kompisen
a friend   the friend

↘ ↗ ↘ ↗
en invandrare invandraren
an immigrant the immigrant

C Notice however that the verb accents often change through
the paradigm

↗ .   ↗   ↗   ↗   ↗
läsa   **läs!**   **läser**   **läste**   **läst**
read   read   reads   read   read

↘ ↗   ↗   ↗   ↗   ↘↗
dricka **drick!** **dricker** **drack**   **druckit**
drink   drink   drinks   drank   drunk

Chapter 3

Nouns

Gender and noun type

| **3.1.1** | *Gender* |

Swedish nouns are divided into non-neuter gender (sometimes called *en*-words or N-words or common gender) and neuter gender (sometimes called *ett*-words or T-words). This division is expressed in the choice of the indefinite article (see 3.2.1):

Non-neuter		Neuter	
en bil	**en flicka**	**ett hus**	**ett äpple**
a car	a girl	a house	an apple

Gender determines the end (definite) article singular and plural (see also 3.5.1 f):

	Non-neuter		Neuter	
Singular	**bilen**	**flickan**	**huset**	**äpplet**
	the car	the girl	the house	the apple
Plural	**bilarna**	**flickorna**	**husen**	**äpplena**
	the cars	the girls	the houses	the apples

Gender is also important for the selection of a plural ending (see 3.2.2 ff) and for the agreement of pronouns, adjectives and past participles (see 4.1, 4.2.4, 7.3.2):

huset är stort
the house is big

flickan är stor⊗
the girl is big

ett grönt äpple
a green apple

en stor⊗ flicka
a big girl

⊗ indicates that the adjective takes no ending ('zero ending').

3.1.2 | Gender rules

Gender is only partly predictable for Swedish: the meaning or form (often suffixes) of some nouns may tell us whether we are dealing with a non-neuter or neuter noun, but in many cases we cannot predict gender accurately by either form or meaning. What follows is a guide to those clues available to us for predicting gender by the meaning or form of a word:

1 Non-neuter by meaning:

(a) Most human beings: **en far, en lärare**
Exceptions: ett barn, ett biträde, ett geni

(b) Most animals: **en fisk, en höna**
Exceptions: ett djur, ett får, ett bi, ett lejon

(c) Days, parts of the day: **en fredag, en timme**
Exception: ett dygn

(e) Months, seasons: **januari var kall; hösten, våren**

(f) Trees, flowers, shrubs: **granen, apeln, rosen**
Exceptions: ett träd or compounds in -träd

2 Non-neuter by form are nouns ending in:

-a	**en gata, en krona, en människa** *Exceptions*: ett drama, ett öga
-are	**en lärare, en stockholmare** *Exception*: ett altare
-dom	**en sjukdom, kristendomen**
-else	**en rörelse, en styrelse** *Exception*: ett fängelse
-het	**en svaghet, en personlighet**
-ing/-ning	**en parkering, en höjning**
-ion	**en station, en religion**
-ism	**realismen, socialismen**
-nad	**en byggnad, tystnaden**
-or	**en dator, en agitator**

33

3 Neuter by meaning:

(a) Continents: **Asien är överbefolkat.**   Asia is overpopulated.

(b) Countries: **Sverige är glesbefolkat.**   Sweden is sparsely populated.

(c) Provinces: **Norrland är kallt.**   Norrland is cold.

(d) Towns: **Stockholm är stort.**   Stockholm is big.

Notice the 'hidden agreement' in these four cases where there is no article on the noun to indicate gender.

(e) Letters of the alphabet: **ett a, ett b**

(f) Nouns from other parts of speech: **nuet, jaget, ett nej**

4 Neuter by form are nouns ending in:

-ande	**ett antagande**
	Exceptions: people – en sökande, en studerande
-ende	**ett leende, ett utseende**
-um	**ett faktum, ett museum, ett gymnasium**

3.1.3 Types of noun

The three main types of noun are:

1   Common nouns: **katt** (cat), **stol** (chair), **pojke** (boy)
2   Abstract nouns: **glädje** (joy), **sjukdom** (illness), **mjukhet** (softness)
3   Proper nouns: **Gustav, Stockholm, Sverige** (Sweden), **Volvo**

A further important distinction is made between count nouns and non-count nouns (see also 3.4.1, 4.5.7 (3)):

Count nouns are often concrete things and creatures:

   bulle (bun), **träd** (tree), **student** (student)

Some abstracts are count nouns: **skratt** (laugh), **färg** (colour)

Non-count nouns are often substances:

   vatten (water), **bensin** (petrol), **luft** (air)

Some abstracts are non-count nouns: **vithet** (whiteness), **lycka** (happiness)

Indefinite forms

Swedish has indefinite and definite forms of the noun. The indefinite singular form is often indicated by the use of the indefinite article – either **en** or **ett** – before the noun, depending on the gender of the noun:

Non-neuter	**en mor**	a mother	For constructions with
	en timme	an hour	adjectives, see 4.1–4.3.6 ff.
Neuter	**ett hus**	a house	
	ett äpple	an apple	

As in English a whole species or family may be denoted by either definite singular or indefinite plural:

Ekorrar/Ekorren finns överallt i Europa.

Squirrels are/The squirrel is found throughout Europe.

The indefinite article is the same as the numeral **en, ett**, 'one'. The indefinite plural of Swedish nouns is formed by adding one of several different endings to the noun, see 3.2.2 ff.

3.2.2 *Plurals*

Regular plurals are expressed by the addition of one of the following endings:

-or -ar -er -r -n ⊗**/zero** (ie. no plural ending) **-s**

Nouns are often grouped by their plural ending in declensions which correspond to these endings:

Declension

1	**en gata**	a street	**två gator**	two streets
2	**en sjö**	a lake	**två sjöar**	two lakes
3	**en park**	a park	**två parker**	two parks
4	**en sko**	a shoe	**två skor**	two shoes
5	**ett yrke**	a profession	**två yrken**	two professions
6	**ett barn**	a child	**två barn**⊗	two children
7	**en sprinkler**	a sprinkler	**två sprinklers**	two sprinklers

Plurals of Swedish nouns are very largely predictable. The decisive factors in the choice of a plural ending are:

1 Gender – Whether it is a non-neuter or neuter noun:

en arm	två arm*ar*	ett hus	två hus⊗
en krona	två kron*or*	ett stycke	två stycke*n*

2 Whether the neuter noun ends in a vowel or a consonant:

ett kvitto	två kvitto*n*	ett hus	två hus⊗
ett parti	två parti*er*		

3 Whether the neuter noun ending in a vowel has stress on the last syllable:

ett 'ställe	två ställe*n*	ett bage'r$\underline{i}$	två bageri*er*

4 Whether the non-neuter noun has stress on the last syllable:

en sta'ti$\underline{o}$n	två station*er*

5 Which of the following suffixes the non-neuter noun without stress on the last syllable possesses:

-e	en pojke	två pojk*ar*
-a	en krona	två kron*or*
-ande	en studerande	två studerande⊗
-are	en läkare	två läkare⊗
-er	en indier	två indier⊗
-(n)ing	en tidning	två tidning*ar*
-tion	en lektion	två lektion*er*
-het	en nyhet	två nyhet*er*
-nad	en byggnad	två byggnad*er*

3.2.3 below shows these factors both as rules and in diagrammatic form.

| 3.2.3 | *Plurals – predictability* |

There are six main rules for predicting the plural forms of nouns:

1 Non-neuter nouns ending in unstressed -a have a plural in **-or** (and drop -a).

en flicka   **två flickor**

2 Non-neuter nouns ending in unstressed -e have a plural in **-ar** (and drop -e).

en pojke   **två pojkar**

3 Non-neuter nouns with stress on the last syllable have a plural in **-er**.

 en armé   **två arméer**

4 Neuter nouns ending in a stressed vowel have a plural in **-er**.

ett geni   **två genier**

5 Neuter nouns ending in an unstressed vowel have a plural in **-n**.

ett yrke   **två yrken**

6 Neuter nouns ending in a consonant have a plural in **-zero** (ie. no plural ending, shown below as ⊗).

ett barn   **två barn⊗**

It is possible to formulate a number of additional rules for prediction:

7 Non-neuter nouns ending in suffix **-are, -ande** have a plural in **-zero**.

en lärare   **två lärare⊗**

en sökande   **två sökande⊗**

8 Non-neuter nouns ending in suffix **-er** have a plural in **-zero**.

en tekniker   **två tekniker⊗**

9 Nouns (always non-neuter) ending in suffix **-(n)ing** have a plural in **-ar**.

en tidning   **två tidningar**

10 Nouns (always non-neuter) ending in the stressed suffixes **-het, -nad, -ion** have a plural in -er.

en nyhet	**två nyheter**
en byggnad	**två bygnader**
en station	**två stationer**

Notes:

1 It is often difficult to predict the plurals of monosyllabic non-neuter nouns ending in a consonant. Such nouns add *either* -ar *or* -er:

en bil	**två bil*ar***
en färg	**två färg*er***
en hund	**två hund*ar***
en park	**två park*er***

2 Nouns ending in -el, -en, -er tend to add -ar after dropping the -e of the final syllable:

en fågel	**två fågl*ar***
en vinter	**två vintr*ar***
en fröken	**två frökn*ar***

Notice, however, that some loanwords take -er:

en muskel	**två muskl*er***
en fiber	**två fibr*er***

Plural predictability chart

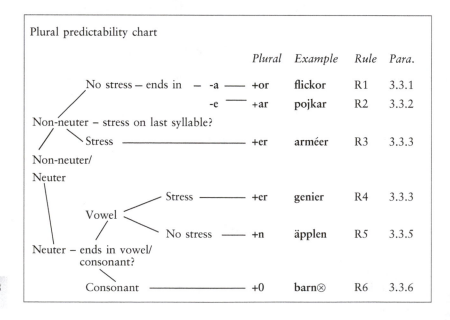

	Plural	Example	Rule	Para.
No stress — ends in — -a — +or		flickor	R1	3.3.1
-e — +ar		pojkar	R2	3.3.2
Non-neuter – stress on last syllable? Stress — +er		arméer	R3	3.3.3
Non-neuter/ Neuter — Vowel — Stress — +er		genier	R4	3.3.3
No stress — +n		äpplen	R5	3.3.5
Neuter – ends in vowel/ consonant? Consonant — +0		barn⊗	R6	3.3.6

3.3 Plural forms

Whilst plurals in the majority of cases are predictable from the form or pronunciation of the noun (see 3.2.2 ff), it is also useful to gather nouns into groups (often called 'declensions') according to their plural ending:

3.3.1 Plurals in -or (first declension)

These comprise only non-neuter nouns, which include:

1 Virtually all nouns of two or more syllables ending in -a. These drop the -a before adding the plural ending:

en blomma	+*or*	→ två blommor	flower(s)
en människa	+*or*	→ två människor	person(s)

2 Very few others:

en toffel	+*or*	→ två tofflor	slipper(s)
en ros	+*or*	→ två rosor	rose(s)

3.3.2 Plurals in -ar (second declension)

These comprise only non-neuter nouns, which include:

1 Most monosyllabic nouns ending in a consonant:

en hund	+*ar*	→ två hundar	dog(s)
en arm	+*ar*	→ två armar	arm(s)

2 Some monosyllabic nouns ending in a vowel:

en sjö	+*ar*	→ två sjöar	lake(s)
en å	+*ar*	→ två åar	river(s)

3 Nouns ending in unstressed -e. These drop the -e before adding the plural ending:

en pojke	+*ar*	→ två pojkar	boy(s)

39

4 Many nouns ending in unstressed -en, -el, -er. These drop the -e of the last syllable before adding the plural ending:

| en fågel | +*ar* | → två fåglar | bird(s) |
| en vinter | +*ar* | → två vintrar | winter(s) |

5 Many nouns ending in -(n)ing:

| en övning | +*ar* | → två övningar | exercise(s) |
| en tävling | +*ar* | → två tävlingar | competition(s) |

6 Notice the following irregular nouns:

en dotter	+*ar*	→ två döttrar	daughter(s)
en mo(de)r	+*ar*	→ två mödrar	mother(s)
en mun	+*ar*	→ två munnar	mouth(s)
en morgon	+*ar*	→ två morgnar	morning(s)
en sommar	+*ar*	→ två somrar	summer(s)

7 Notice there is one neuter noun:

| ett finger | +*ar* | → två fingrar | finger(s) |

3.3.3 | *Plurals in -er (third declension)*

These comprise both non-neuter and neuter nouns, which include:

1 Some monosyllabic non-neuter nouns ending in a consonant:

| en park | +*er* | → två parker | park(s) |
| en färg | +*er* | → två färger | colour(s) |

2 Many nouns of both genders with stress on the final syllable (often loans):

en miljö	+*er*	→ två miljöer	environment(s)
en restaurang	+*er*	→ två restauranger	restaurant(s)
en student	+*er*	→ två studenter	student(s)
ett myteri	+*er*	→ två myterier	mutiny (mutinies)

3 Some nouns ending in unstressed -en, -el, -er. These drop the -e of the last syllable before adding the plural ending:

en möbel	**+er**	→	**två möbler**	piece(s) of furniture
en fiber	**+er**	→	**två fibrer**	fibre(s)

4 A number of nouns which change their root vowel:

A → Ä:	**en hand**	**+er**	→	**två händer**	hand(s)
	en tand	**+er**	→	**två tänder**	tooth (teeth)
	en strand	**+er**	→	**två stränder**	beach(es)
	ett land	**+er**	→	**två länder**	country (countries)
	en stad	**+er**	→	**två städer**	town(s)
O →Ö:	**en son**	**+er**	→	**två söner**	son(s)
	en ledamot	**+er**	→	**två ledamöter**	member(s)

O → Ö + *vowel shortening*:

en fot	**+er**	→	**två fötter**	foot (feet)
en bok	**+er**	→	**två böcker**	book(s)
en rot	**+er**	→	**två rötter**	root(s)

3.3.4 Plurals in -r (fourth declension)

These comprise mostly non-neuter nouns ending in a vowel, which include:

1 Nouns ending in -e, -ie, -je, -else, -arie:

en linje	**+r**	→	**två linjer**	line(s)
en bakelse	**+r**	→	**två bakelser**	cream cake(s)
ett fängelse	**+r**	→	**två fängelser**	prison(s)
en bibliotekarie	**+r**	→	**två bibliotekarier**	librarian(s)
Notice: **en bonde**	**+r**	→	**två bönder**	farmer(s)

41

2 Some nouns ending in -o, -u, -å, -ö:

en sko	+r	→ två skor	shoe(s)
en tå	+r	→ två tår	toe(s)

3.3.5 | Plurals in -n (fifth declension)

1 These comprise only neuter nouns ending in an unstressed vowel:

ett hjärta	+n	→ två hjärtan	heart(s)
ett ansikte	+n	→ två ansikten	face(s)
ett meddelande	+n	→ två meddelanden	message(s)
ett leende	+n	→ två leenden	smile(s)
ett bi	+n	→ två bin	bee(s)
ett konto	+n	→ två konton	account(s)

2 Notice the following irregular -n plurals:

ett öga	→ två ögon	eye(s)
ett öra	→ två öron	ear(s)
ett huvud	→ två huvuden	head(s)

3.3.6 | Plurals in -zero (no plural ending, sixth declension)

These comprise both neuter and non-neuter nouns, which include:

1 Many neuter nouns ending in a consonant:

ett hus	+zero	→ två hus⊗	house(s)
ett barn	+zero	→ två barn⊗	child(ren)
ett fönster	+zero	→ två fönster⊗	window(s)

2 Most non-neuter nouns ending in -are, -er, -ande, -ende denoting people and professions:

en läkare	+zero	→ två läkare⊗	doctor(s)
en studerande	+zero	→ två studerande⊗	student(s)

| en musiker | +zero | → två musiker⊗ | musician(s) |
| en gående | +zero | → två gående⊗ | pedestrian(s) |

3 A few non-neuter nouns with vowel change in the plural:

en man	+zero	→ två män⊗	man (men)
en bro(de)r	+zero	→ två bröder⊗	brother(s)
en mus	+zero	→ två möss⊗	mouse (mice)
en gås	+zero	→ två gäss⊗	goose (geese)

4 Nouns of measurement of both genders:

en kilometer	+zero	→ två kilometer⊗	kilometre(s)
en mil	+zero	→ två mil⊗	Swedish mile(s)
ett ton	+zero	→ två ton⊗	tonne(s)
en liter	+zero	→ två liter⊗	litre(s)

5 Some Latin and Greek loanwords of both genders possess alternative Swedish plurals in zero (marked ⊗):

ett centrum	två centrum⊗/centrer/centra	centre(s)
ett faktum	två faktum⊗/fakta	fact(s)
ett lexikon	två lexikon⊗/lexika	dictionary (dictionaries)

3.3.7 | Plurals in -s (seventh declension)

The plural in -s is used with many non-neuter loanwords that retain their foreign character but do not have stress on the final syllable:

en happening +s → **två happenings**

When the loan becomes familiar in Swedish a Swedish plural often replaces the -s:

en reporter → **två reportrar**

Many such nouns are rarely found in the singular:

pickels, cornflakes, shorts

When forming the definite plural, the -s ending is regarded as if it were part of the stem, and the noun treated as if it had a zero plural with **-en** being added:

jeansen the jeans

3.3.8 | Collective nouns

A few nouns have special collective non-count forms. These include

Singular	Plural	Collective plural
ärta	**ärtor**	**ärter**
mygga	**myggor**	**mygg**
polis	**poliser**	**polis**
man	**män**	**man/mannar**

Examples:

två ärtor på min tallrik	two peas on my plate
ärter med fläsk	peas with pork
tre myggor på handen	three mosquitoes on my hand
mycket mygg i fjällen	a lot of mosquitoes in the mountains
Poliserna/polisen kom i flera bilar.	The police arrived in several cars.
Det satt tre män utanför.	Three men sat outside.
en officer och trettio man	an officer and 30 men

3.3.9 | Nouns with no plural form or no singular form

1 Nouns with no plural form comprise:

(a) Nouns which, because of their meaning, possess no plural form:

Abstract nouns: **fattigdom**, poverty; **glädje**, joy; **köld**, cold

Some names of substances: **guld**, gold; **snö**, snow; **kol**, coal;
                              luft, air

Some collective nouns: **boskap**, cattle; **folk**, people

(b) Non-neuter nouns ending in unstressed -**an** which occasionally 'borrow' a plural from other synonymous words:

en önskan	två önskningar	wish
en början	två inledningar	introduction
en tävlan	två tävlingar	competition
en anmälan	två anmälningar	report

2 Nouns with no singular form include:

1 decl. **sopor**, rubbish; **byxor**, trousers
2 decl. **pengar**, money
3 decl. **grönsaker**, vegetables; **kalsonger**, underpants; **kläder**, clothes
5 decl. **glasögon**, spectacles; **hängslen**, braces
6 decl. **livsmedel**, groceries
7 decl. **shorts**, jeans

3.4 Differences in number between Swedish and English

3.4.1 Differences in number

Swedish may have a plural where English has a singular and vice versa:

1 Non-count singular in English, count plural in Swedish:

advice	råd	furniture	möbler
business	affärer	news	nyheter
income	inkomst(er)	applause	applåder
information	upplysningar	homework	läxor
knowledge	kunskap(er)	cash	kontanter
money	pengar		

2 Count plural in English, often non-count singular in Swedish:

| contents | innehåll | stairs | trappa |
| drugs | narkotika, knark | spirits | sprit |

Note: **en nyhet** a piece of news, **en möbel** a piece of furniture

45

3 Count plural in English, count singular in Swedish:

scissors	**(en) sax**	scales	**(en) våg**
tweezers	**(en) pincett**	pincers	**(en) tång**

Note: These Swedish nouns also have plural forms (**två saxar, pincetter, vågar, tänger**) corresponding to, for example, two pairs of scissors.

3.5 Definite declension

3.5.1 | Forms with end article singular

The definite form of the noun is indicated by the use of the end (definite) article, **-en** for singular non-neuter nouns, **-et** for singular neuter nouns (cf. indefinite **en, ett,** 3.2.1). If a noun ends in a vowel the end article is **-n** or **-t**. The end article in Swedish is not a separate word but a suffix which is added to the end of the noun:

	Indefinite		Definite (Form with end article)
a car	**en bil**	the car	**bilen**
a house	**ett hus**	the house	**huset**

The form of the noun with end article singular (ie. the singular definite) can be predicted from the gender and ending of the noun as shown in the following rules:

1 Non-neuter ending in a consonant: arm   *+en* → armen
(other than **-l** or **-r**)

2 Non-neuter ending in a vowel   flicka   *+n* → flickan
(stressed or unstressed):   industri̱   *+n* → industrin

3 Non-neuter ending in an unstressed   fågel   *+n* → fågeln
vowel **+l/r**:   moder   *+n* → modern
    doktor   *+n* → doktorn

4 Neuter ending in a consonant: hus   *+et* → huset

5 Neuter ending in an unstressed vowel: yrke   *+t* → yrket

6 Neuter ending in a stressed vowel:　　　**geni**　　**+et** → geniet

Notice that the stem of the following nouns in -el, -en, -er drops an -e
before adding the end article:

öken	+*en*	→ öknen
tecken	+*en*	→ tecknen
exempel	+*et*	→ exemplet
finger	+*et*	→ fingret

Notice that neuters ending in **-eum**, **-ium** drop the letters **-um** before
adding the end article:

museum +*et* → museet

Notice also some short forms in spoken Swedish that are increasingly
found in written Swedish:

stan (from **staden**), **dan** (from **dagen**), **sommarn** (from
sommaren), **knät** (from **knäet**), **idén** (from **idéen**), **direktörn**
(from **direktören**), **lärarn** (from **läraren**)

Nouns – forms with end article singular – predictability chart

	ends in a consonant ———————— +en armen	Rule 1
	(*Exceptions:* l, r)	
Non-neuter–ends in a *vowel* ———————— +n industrin	Rule 2
	`ends in an *unstressed vowel* +l, r – +n fågeln	Rule 3
Non-neuter/Neuter?		
	ends in a *consonant* ———————— +et huset	Rule 4
Neuter		
	unstressed ———— +t yrket	Rule 5
	ends in a *vowel*	
	stressed ———— +et geniet	Rule 6

3.5.2 | *Forms with end article plural*

The end article plural is either **-na, -a,** or **-en.** The form of the noun with
end article plural (ie. plural definite) can be predicted from the following
rules (see also 3.2.3 for plural forms):

1 Plurals ending in a **vowel + r** (both genders):

flickor	**+na**	→ **flickorna**
armar	**+na**	→ **armarna**

filmer	**+na**	→ **filmerna**
viner	**+na**	→ **vinerna**

Notice that plurals of nouns in -are drop the final -e:

arbetare	**+na**	→ **arbetarna**
läkare	**+na**	→ **läkarna**

2 Plurals ending in a **consonant other than -r** (both genders):

hus	**+en**	→ **husen**
män	**+en**	→ **männen**

Notice that stems of polysyllabic nouns in -el, -en, -er drop an -e:

exempel	**+en**	→ **exemplen**
tecken	**+en**	→ **tecknen**
fönster	**+en**	→ **fönstren**

3 Plurals of neuter nouns ending in a vowel which have added +n to form their plural:

yrken	**+a**	→ **yrkena**

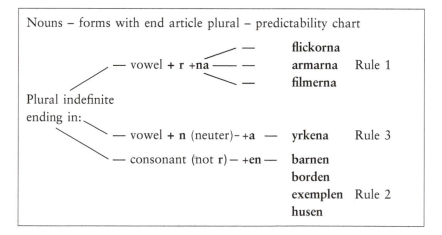

Nouns – forms with end article plural – predictability chart

Plural indefinite ending in:
- vowel + r +na
  - — flickorna
  - — armarna — Rule 1
  - — filmerna
- vowel + n (neuter)- +a — yrkena — Rule 3
- consonant (not r)- +en — barnen
  - borden
  - exemplen — Rule 2
  - husen

3.6 Article use

In many cases usage is similar in the two languages, e.g. both use definite articles for familiar ideas and indefinite articles for new ideas. The paragraphs below outline major *differences* in usage.

3.6.1 | *End article in Swedish, no article in English*

1 Abstract nouns and nouns in a general sense:

Svenskarna älskar naturen.	Swedes love nature.
Historien upprepar sig.	History repeats itself.
Sådant är livet.	Such is life.
Han fruktar döden.	He fears death.
Priserna stiger jämt.	Prices are always rising.

2 Locations:

Olle går i kyrkan/skolan.	Olle goes to church/school.
Eva åker till staden.	Eva is going to town.
Eva är i staden.	Eva is in town.
Lars studerar vid universitetet.	Lars is (studying) at university.

3 Days, seasons, festivals, mealtimes:

På fredagarna åker vi bort.	On Fridays we go away.
På vintern spelar de ishockey.	In winter they play ice hockey.
Vi ses på nyårsdagen!	Be seeing you on New Year's Day!
Efter middagen läste jag en bok.	After dinner I read a book.

See also 10.3.3.

3.6.2 *End article in Swedish, indefinite article in English*

1 Prices:

Osten kostar 130 kronor kilot.
The cheese costs 130 kronor a kilo.

2 Frequency of occurrence:

Jag tjänar 500 kronor i timmen, dvs 4000 kronor om dagen.
I earn 500 kronor an hour, i.e. 4,000 kronor a day.

 3.6.3 *No article in Swedish, definite article in English*

1 Instruments, machines:

Han spelar piano.	He is playing the piano.
De lyssnar på radio.	They are listening to the radio.
Vi tittar på tv.	We are watching (the) TV.

2 Proper names:

Vi är bjudna till Janssons ikväll.
We have been invited to the Janssons tonight.

3 Nouns after **nästa, samma, fel, rätt, följande, föregående** (cf. 4.3.3 (6)):

De bor i nästa hus.	They live in the next house.
Samma dag kom vi hem.	The same day we came home.
Det var rätt/fel hus.	It was the right/wrong house.
Gör det på följande sätt!	Do it in the following way.

3.6.4 *No article in Swedish, indefinite article in English*

1 Nationality, profession, religious and political belief:

Per är norrman.	Per is a Norwegian.
Han är lärare.	He is a teacher.
Moberg var socialist.	Moberg was a socialist.
Hon är katolik.	She is a Catholic.

Exceptions:

(a) When the noun is qualified by an adjective:

Hon är en god katolik.   She is a good Catholic.

(b) When the noun is preceded by a preposition:

Hon är gift med en lärare.   She is married to a teacher.

(c) When the noun is qualified by a relative clause:

Hon är en lärare som kan sin sak.   She is a teacher who knows her stuff.

2 In many idiomatic expressions with a singular count noun, when only one is obvious and inferred:

De väntar barn och söker bostad/lägenhet.
They are expecting a child and looking for somewhere to live/a flat.

Hon har inte körkort/bil.
She has not got a driving licence/a car.

Han var utan arbete.
He was without a job.

3 Nouns with the words **vilken, hur ... än**:

Vilken skön dag!
What a beautiful day!

Hur fint hus de än har, är det inte lika bra som vårt.
However nice a house they may have, it is not as nice as ours.

| 3.6.5 | *End article in Swedish, possessive pronoun in English* |

Parts of the body, clothing:

Hon skall tvätta håret/händerna.
She is going to wash her hair/hands.

Hon tog av sig skorna/kappan.
She took off her shoes/coat.

Han har ont i ryggen/magen.
He has a pain in his back/stomach.

| 3.6.6 | *Article use with demonstrative pronouns* |

Den här etc. + End article	*Den* etc. + End article	*Denna* etc. No end article
See also 5.8.		
Non-neuter **den här filmen** **den där filmen** this/that film	**den filmen** this/that film	**denna film**⊗ this/that film
Neuter **det här kortet** **det där kortet** this/that card	**det kortet** this/that card	**detta kort**⊗ this/that card
Plural **de här filmerna** **de där filmerna** these/those films	**de filmerna** these/those films	**dessa filmer**⊗ these/those films
de här korten **de där korten** these/those cards	**de korten** these/those cards	**dessa kort**⊗ these/those cards

Exception: where **den/det/de** are determinative pronouns, see 5.9.

| 3.6.7 | **No article after the possessive** |

As in English, nouns following a possessive **never** take a definite article (see also 5.5):

| **pennan** | the pen | **min penna** | my pen |
| **bordet** | the table | **mitt bord** | my table |

This also applies to constructions with noun + adjective (see also 4.3.3):

| **min röda penna** | my red pen |
| **mitt stora bord** | my big table |

3.7 Genitives

3.7.1 | *The genitive*

See 10.3.5 for the translation of English expressions with 'of'.

1 The Swedish genitive is formed by adding -s to the noun. Notice that there is no apostrophe:

en flickas	**flickans**	**flickors**	**flickornas**
a girl's	the girl's	girls'	the girls'

Exceptions

(a) No -s after a noun ending in -s, -x:

Marx skrifter   Marx's writings

en kaktus taggar   a cactus's spines

(b) No -s after place names ending in a vowel:

Uppsala slott   Uppsala Castle
(cf. **Gripsholms slott**)

2 Latin genitive endings are found in some names:

Jesu liv (← Jesus)   Jesus's life

Kristi himmelsfärd (← Kristus)   Christ's ascension

3 The genitive -s is usually placed on the last word of the group:

mannen på gatans åsikter   the views of the man in the street

Karl den tolftes död   the death of Charles XII

4 The noun following a genitive *never* takes an end article:

gårdens ägare⊗   *the* owner of the farm

Sveriges huvdstad⊗   *the* capital of Sweden

årets sista dag⊗   *the* last day of the year

5 In addition to denoting possession or belonging in a wide sense, the genitive is also used in the following senses:

(a) In measurement:

ett par timmars sömn	a couple of hours' sleep
ett fyrtifem minuters program	a 45-minute programme

(b) To express 'a kind (sort) of':

en sorts fisk	a kind of fish
alla sorters mat	all kinds of food
ett slags fisk	a kind of fish
alla slags mat	all kinds of food

(c) In names:

Jag handlar alltid hos Olssons.	I always shop at Olsson's.
Vi bor mitt emot Perssons.	We live opposite Persson's.

(d) In some old genitive case endings which remain in a few set phrases after **till**:

gå till fots/skogs/bords/sängs	go on foot/into the forest/to table/to bed
gå till väga	set about (something)
vara till salu/till låns	be for sale/on loan

Chapter 4

Adjectives

4.1 Adjectives in outline

Swedish adjectives inflect. In the indefinite declension they agree with the noun in gender (singular only) and in number both attributively and predicatively. They also add inflexional endings in the definite declension.

Indefinite forms

	Non-neuter	Neuter	Plural
Attributive	**en stor⊗ bil**	**ett stort hus**	**stora bilar/hus**
	a big car	a big house	big cars/houses
	god⊗ mat	**varmt vatten**	**raka vägar**
	good food	hot water	straight roads
Predicative	**bilen är stor⊗**	**huset är stort**	**bilarna/husen är stora**
	the car is big	the house is big	the cars/houses are big

Definite forms

den stora bilen	**det stora huset**	**de stora bilarna/husen**
the big car	the big house	the big cars/houses

Notes:

1 For the inflexion of adjectives and past participles, see 4.2.1 ff, 7.3.1.

2 An alternative form of the adjective, in -e, is sometimes found in the definite singular before non-neuter nouns that clearly indicate a male person (cf. 4.3.1 (2)). This form is more frequent in non-fiction and formal prose, and today occurs only rarely in spoken Swedish except in southern Sweden:

den gamle mannen	the old man
den store ledaren Napoleon	the great leader Napoleon

3 The definite ending in -e also occurs, as a compulsory form, on the adjective ending in -ad, superlative in -ast (cf. 4.3.1 (2)):

den nymålade stugan   the newly painted cottage

det billigaste huset   the cheapest house

4.2 Indefinite declension

4.2.1 Indefinite forms – regular

Main rule: Most adjectives including all those that end in -(l)ig add -t in the neuter form and -a in the plural (non-neuter and neuter):

Non-neuter	Neuter	Plural
+⊗ *(no ending)*	+*t*	+*a*
en fin⊗ tavla	**ett fint hus**	**fina tavlor/hus**
a fine picture	a fine house	fine pictures/houses
en rolig⊗ film	**ett roligt skämt**	**roliga filmer/skämt**
a funny film	a funny joke	funny films/jokes

4.2.2 Indefinite forms – variations

Non-neuter	Neuter	Plural

Adjectives ending in:

1 *long vowel*	*short vowel*	*long vowel*	
	+*tt*	+*a*	
fri	**fritt**	**fria**	free
rå	**rått**	**råa**	raw

Like **fri**: **ny** (new), **slö** (blunt)

Note that **blå** (blue) and **grå** (grey) have optional plural forms: **blå/blåa**, **grå/gråa**.

2 *long vowel*	*short vowel*	*long vowel*	
+*t*	+*tt*	+*t+a*	
vit	**vitt**	**vita**	white

Like **vit**: **het** (hot), **fet** (fat), **våt** (wet)

Note that many loanwords in *long vowel* +*t* do not add an extra -t in the neuter form: **akut, desperat, diskret, konkret, privat, separat**, etc.

3	*short vowel*	*short vowel*	*short vowel*	
	+*tt*	+*tt*	+*tt+a*	
	lätt	**lätt**	**lätta**	easy

Like lätt: **rätt** (right), **trött** (tired), **mätt** (replete)

4	*consonant*	*consonant*	*consonant*	
	+*t*	+*t*	+*t+a*	
	exakt	**exakt**	**exakta**	exact

Like exakt: **abstrakt, elegant, intelligent, intressant, perfekt**

This group also includes some indigenous monosyllabic adjectives: **brant** (steep), **fast** (firm), **kort** (short), **stolt** (proud), **tyst** (silent).

5	*long vowel*	*short vowel*	*long vowel*	
	+*d*	+*tt*	+*d+a*	
	glad	**glatt**	**glada**	happy

Like glad: **bred** (wide), **död** (dead), **god** (good), **röd** (red)

6	*consonant*	*consonant*	*consonant*	
	+*d*	+*t*	+*d+a*	
	hård	**hårt**	**hårda**	hard

Like hård: **ond** (evil), **vild** (wild), **mild** (mild), **värd** (worth), and past participles of second conjugation (IIa) verbs: **stängd** (closed), **berömd** (famous), **bestämd** (definite)

7	*-ad*	*-at*	*-ad+e*	
	älskad	**älskat**	**älskade**	loved

Like älskad: all first conjugation past participles, e.g. **kortfattad** (concise), **koncentrerad** (concentrated). See 7.3.2.

8	*short vowel*	*short vowel*	*short vowel*	
	+*m*	+*m+t*	+*mm+a*	
	dum	**dumt**	**dumma**	stupid

Like dum: **tom** (empty), **grym** (cruel), **hjälpsam** (helpful), **långsam** (slow), **våldsam** (violent). See 14.2.

9	*short vowel*	*short vowel*	*short vowel*	
	+*nn*	+*n+t*	+*nn+a*	
	sann	**sant**	**sanna**	true

Like sann: **grann** (pretty), **noggrann** (careful), **tunn** (thin). See 14.2.

10 *-el/-er*	*-el+t/-er+t*	*-l+a/-r+a*	
enkel	**enkelt**	**enkla**	simple
vacker	**vackert**	**vackra**	pretty

Like **enkel**: **acceptabel** (acceptable), **flexibel** (flexible)

Like **vacker**: **säker** (sure), **mager** (thin), **nykter** (sober)

11 *-en*	*-e+t*	*-n+a*	
mogen	**moget**	**mogna**	ripe
skriven	**skrivet**	**skrivna**	written

Like **mogen**: **egen** (own), **ledsen** (sad), **nyfiken** (curious), **öppen** (open), **vaken** (awake), **erfaren** (experienced) and past participles of fourth conjugation verbs. See 7.3.1 f.

12 **gammal**	**gammalt**	**gamla**	old

13 **liten**	**litet**	**små**	little

The definite forms (see 4.1) of **liten** are **lilla** (non-neuter/neuter) and **små** (plural).

4.2.3 | Indeclinable adjectives

Some adjectives do not inflect in either definite or indefinite declension, unlike those in 4.2.1 f. These include those ending in -s, -e, -a and some others:

1 Adjectives ending in -s:

These are historically noun genitives.

> **ett medelålders biträde**   a middle-aged assistant

Includes: **gammaldags** (old-fashioned), **stackars** (poor), **utrikes** (foreign), **avsides** (remote).

Exceptions:	adjectives ending in -**ös**:	**nervös**	**nervöst**	**nervösa**	nervous
	adjectives ending in -**is**:	**vis**	**vist**	**visa**	wise

2 Adjectives ending in -e:

ett öde hus   a deserted house

Includes: **främmande** (foreign), **gyllene** (golden), **ense** (agreed), **ordinarie** (regular) and all present participles and comparatives in -are, -re:

omfattande kunskaper   wide knowledge

ett större hus   a bigger house

3 Adjectives ending in -a:

ett bra tag   a good while

Includes: **sakta** (slow), **stilla** (peaceful), **äkta** (genuine), **extra** (extra), **samma** (the same), **nästa** (the next), **förra** ((the) last), **nutida** (present day)

4 Some indeclinable adjectives are only used attributively:

de stackars flickorna   the poor girls

i fjärran länder   in foreign parts

det dåtida Stockholm   the Stockholm of that time

5 Some indeclinable adjectives are only used predicatively:

Arbetet var slut för dagen.   Work had finished for the day.

Bilen är sönder.   The car is unserviceable.

Jag är ense med dig.   I agree with you.

6 Some indeclinable adjectives may be used either attributively or predicatively:

Jag slog fel nummer.   I dialled the wrong number.

Flera siffror är fel.   Several figures are wrong.

en öde ö   a desert island

Landskapet var helt öde.   The countryside was totally
                                  desolate.

4.2.4 | Indefinite constructions

The indefinite noun phrase (in this case: indefinite premodifier + adjective + noun) usually expresses something general and non-specific.

Non-neuter　　　　*Neuter*　　　　*Plural*

1 When no word precedes adjective + noun:

god⊗ mat　　　　vacker*t* väder　　　　rak*a* vägar

2 When one of the following premodifiers precedes adjective + noun:

en		ett		två		a/two
någon		något		några		a/some/any
ingen		inget		inga		no
en enda		ett enda		–		a single
en annan	stor⊗	ett annat	stor*t*	andra	stor*a*	(an)other
	pojke		hus		pojkar/hus	
en likadan		ett likadant		likadana		(a) similar
en sådan		ett sådant		sådana		such (a)
vilken		vilket		vilka		which
varje		varje		–		each
				många		many
				flera		several
				alla		all
				få		few
				olika		different
				somliga		some
				åtskilliga		several

4.2.5 | Agreement and lack of agreement

Generally speaking Swedish adjectives in the indefinite agree with the noun which they qualify:

Gården är stor⊗, men huset är litet med mörk*a* rum.
The farm is big but the house is small with dark rooms.

Notice, however, the following special cases where there is lack of agreement:

1 Constructions according to meaning:

Folk är mer intresserade av idrott än politik.
People are more interested in sport than politics.

Cf. **lite(t) folk**
few people

Statsrådet var säker på sin sak.
The minister was sure of her case.

Notice also:

laget ... de (the team ... they); **paret ... de** (the couple ... they);
affärsbiträdet ... han/hon (the shop assistant ... he/she); **barnet
... hon/han** (the child ... he/she); **polisen ... de** (the police ...
they)

2 Some nouns used without articles or an additional complement in a
general, abstract or collective sense require the neuter form of the adjective:

Ärter är gott.   Peas are good /to eat/.
Att äta ärter är gott.
Det är gott med ärter.

Danska är svårt.   Danish is difficult.
Att lära sig danska är svårt.
Det är svårt att lära sig danska.

But note:

De här ärterna är goda.   These peas are good.

Hans danska är obegriplig⊗. His Danish is unintelligible.

4.3   Definite declension

4.3.1 | *Definite form of the adjective: -e or -a?*

1 Forms in -a are used:

(a) With non-neuter nouns in the singular: den vackr*a* flickan
                                                den ny*a* stolen

(b) With adjectival nouns in the singular referring to a female person:
                                                den sjuk*a* (damen)

61

(c) With plural nouns of both genders (except those in 2(a), (b) below):

de fin*a* blommorna
de ung*a* pojkarna
de billig*a* husen

(d) With neuter nouns in the singular

det hög*a* trädet

2   Forms in **-e** are used:

(a) With past participles ending in **-ad**:

den nymålad*e* stugan
det nymålad*e* huset
de nymålad*e* husen/stugorna

(b) With superlatives ending in **-ast**: (cf. 4.5.1)

den vackrast*e* flickan
det billigast*e* huset
de billigast*e* husen

(c) With singular nouns that clearly refer to a male person: (*More common form*, see 1(a) above):   den lång*e* pojken

(d) With singular adjectival nouns referring to a male person: (*Compulsory form*, see 4.4.1):   den sjuk*e* (mannen)

Note: **äkta** (genuine, married), **före detta** (former, ex-) have no e-form:

Evas äkta man
Barbros före detta man

Remember: **e**-forms are used with adjectives in **-ad, -ast** and with masculine singulars.

| **4.3.2** | *Definite construction Type I –* **den nya bilen** |

The definite noun phrase (i.e. definite premodifier + adjective + noun) usually expresses something specific (cf. indefinite noun phrase, 4.2.4). This is the basic type of definite construction. The noun is defined by:

(1) the front (adjectival) article: **den, det** or **de**
(2) the definite ending on the adjective: **-a** (or **-e**)
(3) the end article on the noun: **-(e)n, -(e)t, -na, -a** or **-en**

Non-neuter	*Neuter*	*Plural*
den nya bilen	**det nya huset**	**de nya bilarna/husen**
(1) (2) (3)	(1) (2) (3)	(1) (2) (3) (3)
the new car	the new house	the new cars/houses

The construction above is sometimes called 'double definition'. Constructions with the demonstrative **den här**, etc., (see 5.8) are an extension of this type:

den här nya bilen   **det här nya huset**   **de här nya bilarna/husen**
this new car   this new house   these new cars/houses

4.3.3 | *Definite construction Type 2 – firmans nya bil*

In many cases the adjective has a definite ending -a/-e while there is no end article on the noun (cf. 4.3.2). This occurs after the following types of word:

1 The genitive:

Non-neuter	*Neuter*	*Plural*
firmans nya bil	**mannens nya hus**	**barnets nya kompisar**
the firm's new car	the man's new house	the child's new friends
Olles nya bil	**Olles nya hus**	**Olles nya kompisar**
Olle's new car	Olle's new house	Olle's new friends

Note: the genitive of measurement (which takes the indefinite endings in -⊗, -t, -a, 3.7.1):

ett trettiminuters långt program (a 30-minute (long) programme)

2 The possessive:

Non-neuter	*Neuter*	*Plural*
min nya dator	**mitt nya hus**	**mina nya skor**
my new computer	my new house	my new shoes

Exceptions:

1 **egen** takes an indefinite ending after the possessive and genitive:

mammas egen⊗ Olle   Mummy's very own Olle

deras eget fina hus   their own nice house

2 after **var sin/sitt** the adjective may be in either the definite or indefinite form:

Pojkarna fick var sin ny(a) cykel.   The boys each got a new bicycle.

3 The demonstratives **denna, detta, dessa** (cf. **den här**, etc., 5.8):

Non-neuter	*Neuter*	*Plural*
denna mörka skog	**detta vackra träd**	**dessa mörka skogar**
this dark forest	that beautiful tree	these dark forests
		dessa vackra träd
		these beautiful trees

Denna etc., is usually found only in written Swedish.

4 The determinative pronoun **den, det, de** (see 5.9):

De lata studenter som inte pluggade blev underkända i skrivningen.
Those lazy students who did not study failed the exam.

5 The relative pronoun **vars** (see 5.10):

Mannen vars lilla dotter är sjuk, är mycket orolig.
The man whose little daughter is ill is very worried.

Vars is usually found only in written Swedish.

6 Others:

samma	**samma dumma fråga**	the same stupid question
nästa	**nästa vackra helg**	the next fine weekend
följande	**följande svåra problem**	the following difficult problem(s)
föregående	**föregående långa brev**	the previous long letter(s)

4.3.4 | *Definite construction Type 3 – svenska språket*

The front article (cf. 4.3.2) is sometimes omitted:

Non-neuter	*Neuter*	*Plural*
Svenska akademien	Röda korset	Förenta nationerna
the Swedish Academy	the Red Cross	the United Nations

This happens:

1 When an adjectival expression becomes a proper noun and the adjective loses its stress:

Cf.	**det 'vita 'huset**	the white house
	Vita 'huset	the White House (in Washington)

Cf. **det 'röda 'korset**   the red cross

    Röda 'korset   the Red Cross (aid organization)

2 In some cases when a contrast is expressed or implied and the noun is unstressed:

Det är 'stora flickan som fyller år, inte 'lilla flickan.
It is the big girl who is having a birthday, not the little girl.

3 In some cases when the (stressed) adjective provides stylistic marking in the phrase (in spoken Swedish):

Det är ju 'rena smörjan!   That's utter rubbish!

The main kinds of Type 3 construction are found:

(a) In geographical locations:

    Gamla stan   the Old Town

    Döda havet   the Dead Sea

    Förenta staterna   the United States

(b) With nationality adjectives:

    franska revolutionen   the French Revolution

    brittiska flottan   the British navy

(c) With colours:

    gula febern   (the) yellow fever

    Röda halvmånen   the Red Crescent

(d) With words for location:

    på högra sidan   on the right hand side

    i mellersta lådan   in the middle drawer

(e) With compass points:

    södra stambanan   the main (railway) line to the south

    västra halvklotet   the western hemisphere

(f) With ordinal numbers:

första hjälpen	first aid
för andra gången	for the second time

(g) With the words **båda, förra, hela, halva, själva, ena, enda, rena rama, blotta: hela året om** (all year round); **gå halva vägen** (walk half the way); **själva tanken är briljant** (the thought itself is brilliant); **ha ont i ena benet** (have a pain in one leg); **det var rena rama skojet** (it was a complete joke)

4.3.5 | Definite construction Type 4 – första klass

This is a relatively infrequent construction in which there is neither front article nor end article (nor necessarily any word preceding the adjective). It is used:

1 In forms of address and with proper nouns:

Käre far!	Dear father (in letters, for example)
Lilla vän!	My little friend!
gamle herr Nilsson	old Mr Nilsson
Lille Albert	Little Albert

2 With some ordinal numbers and other words denoting position in a series:

Vi ska resa första klass.	We're travelling first class.
De kom i sista stund.	They arrived at the last moment.

3 Often with superlatives:

med största nöje	with great pleasure

4.3.6 | Definite constructions – summary chart

Premodifier:	Non-neuter singular	Neuter singular	Plural

Type 1 – Front article/Demonstrative + end article ('Double definition'). See 4.3.2.

	Non-neuter singular	Neuter singular	Plural
Front article	**den** ⎫	**det** ⎫	**de** ⎫
Demonstrative	**den här** ⎬ **nya bilen**	**det här** ⎬ **nya huset**	**de här** ⎬ **nya bilarna/ husen**
Demonstrative	**den där** ⎭	**det där** ⎭	**de där** ⎭

Type 2 – No end article. See 4.3.3.

	Non-neuter singular	Neuter singular	Plural
Genitive:	**Åkes firmans** ⎫	**Åkes firmans** ⎫	**Åkes firmans** ⎫
Possessive:	**min**	**mitt**	**mina**
Demonstrative:	**denna** ⎬ **nya bil**	**detta** ⎬ **nya hus**	**dessa** ⎬ **nya bilar/ hus**
Determinative:	**den**	**det**	**de**
Relative:	**vars**	**vars**	**vars**
Others:	**samma** **nästa** **följande** **föregående** ⎭	**samma** **nästa** **följande** **föregående** ⎭	**samma** **nästa** **följande** **föregående** ⎭

Type 3 – No front article. See 4.3.4.

	Non-neuter singular	Neuter singular	Plural
In set phrases:	**Gamla testamentet**	**Röda korset**	**Förenta nationerna**
Locations:	**högra sidan**	**Vita huset**	**Klippiga bergen**
Nationality adjectives:	**engelska kyrkan**	**svenska språket**	**Brittiska öarna**
Compass points:	**östra stadsdelen**	**södra korset**	
Ordinal numbers:	**första gången**	**andra steget**	
Certain words:	**hela dagen** **halva kakan**	**förra seklet** **i själva verket** **enda barnet**	

Type 4 – Neither front nor end article. See 4.3.5.

With some forms of address, ordinals and superlatives:

	Käre far! **första klass**	**med största nöje!**

4.4 Adjectival nouns and nationality words

4.4.1 | Adjectival nouns

1 There are three cases where the adjective is used independently, as if it were a noun:

(a) When the noun may easily be supplied: (inflected as an adjective)

Gamla bilar är billigare än nya (bilar).
Old cars are cheaper than new ones.

Ett rött hus och ett vitt (hus).
A red house and a white one.

Alla de äldre (människorna) var trötta.
All the elderly people were tired.

(b) When the noun is not usually supplied. As the examples below show, this is almost invariably when the noun would otherwise describe one or more people, or in cases where the noun **tinget** (= thing) could be supplied. Adjectival nouns of this kind are inflected as adjectives:

en blind (människa)
a blind person

Man bör hjälpa de blinda, de döva och de handikappade.
One should help the blind, the deaf and the disabled.

Notice that, in the singular, the e-form is compulsory in written Swedish for masculines:

den blinde (mannen) cf. **den blinda (kvinnan)** (see 4.3.2)

Det sista han gjorde var att skratta.
The last thing he did was laugh.

Det bästa jag vet är inlagd sill.
The best thing I can think of is pickled herring.

Du är den ende jag älskar.
You are the only one (i.e. the only man) I love.

Du är den enda jag älskar.
You are the only one (i.e. the only woman) I love.

Det enda du kan göra är att vänta.
The only thing you can do is wait.

(c) When the conversion to noun is complete: (inflected as a noun – takes end article)

lillan	the little girl
lillen	the little boy
högern	the Right (in politics)
vänstern	the Left (in politics)

2 As in English, deletion of the noun is common in Swedish in the plural definite:

De unga, de gamla, de sjuka och de fattiga måste hjälpas av de mera välbeställda.
The young, the old, the sick and the poor must be helped by the better off.

But the noun is more often deleted in Swedish, as the number and gender are indicated by the article and adjectival ending:

Cf. 'the tall man' with: **den långe (mannen)**
den långa (kvinnan)
det långa (tinget)
de långa (människorna/tingen)

3 Swedish adjectival nouns can be formed from the following:

(a) The indefinite: **en bekant** (an acquaintance), **en död** (a dead person).

(b) The non-neuter singular definite: **den gamle** (the old man), **den gamla** (the old woman), **den enskilda** (the individual person).

(c) The neuter singular definite: **det nya** (the new thing), **det enda** (the only thing), **det första** (the first thing).

(d) The definite plural: **de kriminella** (the criminal community).

(e) The definite form of the superlative: **det dummaste** (the most stupid thing), **det mest överraskande** (the most surprising thing).

(f) The present participle: **de närvarande** (those present), **den inneboende** (the lodger/inmate), **de överlevande** (the survivors).

(g) The past participle: **en misstänkt** (a suspect), **en nygift** (a newly wed), **en okänd** (a stranger), **den sårade** (the wounded person), **de skadade** (the injured).

4 'The English': Expressions of nationality such as 'the English (people)', 'the French (people)' are rarely translated by adjectival nouns. Common nouns indicating the male inhabitants are used instead (see 4.4.2 below).

The English lost the battle of Hastings.
Engelsmännen förlorade slaget vid Hastings.

The French take their holidays in August.
Fransmännen tar semester i augusti.

4.4.2 | *Nationality words*

Male inhabitant	Female inhabitant	Language	Adjective	Country
I Plurals in **-ar**:	Plurals in **-or**:			
svensk (-ar)	svenska (-or)	svenska	svensk	**Sverige**
dansk (-ar)	danska (-or)	danska	dansk	**Danmark**
tysk (-ar)	tyska (-or)	tyska	tysk	**Tyskland**
islänning (-ar)	isländska (-or)	isländska	isländsk	**Island**
ryss (-ar)	ryska (-or)	ryska	rysk	**Ryssland**
2 Plurals in **-er**:	Plurals in **-or**:			
amerikan (-er)	amerikanska (-or)	engelska	amerikansk	**Amerika**
spanjor (-er)	spanjorska (-or)	spanska	spansk	**Spanien**
kines (-er)	kinesiska (-or)	kinesiska	kinesisk	**Kina**
grek (-er)	grekiska (-or)	grekiska	grekisk	**Grekland**
3 Plurals in ⊗:	Plurals in **-or**:			
engelsman (-män)	engelska (-or)	engelska	engelsk	**England**
fransman (-män)	fransyska (-or)	franska	fransk	**Frankrike**
norrman (-män)	norska (-or)	norska	norsk	**Norge**
finländare	finska (-or)	finska	finsk	**Finland**
holländare	holländska (-or)	holländska	holländsk	**Holland**
italienare	italienska (-or)	italienska	italiensk	**Italien**

4.5   Comparison of adjectives

4.5.1   Comparison with -are, -ast

The comparative has one form only for both genders, definite and indefinite. The superlative has two forms, an indefinite and a definite form. For the definite forms of the superlative see 4.5.6.

A large number of Swedish adjectives form their comparative and superlative forms by adding the endings -are, -ast to the positive form:

Positive	Comparative	Superlative
glad	**gladare**	**gladast**
happy	happier	happiest

This group includes all those adjectives in 4.2.2 (1–6, 8–10) above, including the frequent group ending in -(l)ig:

rolig	**roligare**	**roligast**
funny	funnier	funniest

Notice, however, that some adjectives compared in this way drop the -e in their final syllable before adding -are, -ast (see 4.2.2 (10, 11)):

vacker	**vackrare**	**vackrast**
pretty	prettier	prettiest

Adjectives in a short vowel +m/n (4.2.2 (8)) double the vowel when adding the endings -are, -ast (see 14.2 (3)):

grym	**grymmare**	**grymmast**
cruel	crueller	cruellest

Notice that many adjectives which in English compare with 'more, most' in Swedish add -are, -ast:

Comparative	*Superlative*	
intelligentare	**intelligentast**	more, most intelligent
intressantare	**intressantast**	more, most interesting
modernare	**modernast**	more, most modern
skickligare	**skickligast**	more, most skilful
svårare	**svårast**	more, most difficult

Notes:

1 Past participles in -d, -t tend to compare with **mer(a)**, **mest** or with -are, -ast:
    en mer(a) bortskämd flicka   a more spoiled girl
2 Those adjectives in -d, -dd, -t, -en which resemble past participles tend to add -are, -ast:
    en vidsyntare lärare   a more broad-minded teacher
3 Past participles ending in -en tend to compare with -are, -ast:
    en frusnare brevbärare   a colder postman

4.5.2 Comparison with -re, -st

There is a small group of commonly used monosyllabic adjectives which, with the exception of **hög**, change the stem vowel in the comparative and superlative forms as well as adding -re, -st:

	Positive	Comparative	Superlative	
O → Ö:	**stor**	**större**	**störst**	big, bigger, biggest
	grov	**grövre**	**grövst**	coarse, coarser, coarsest
Å → Ä:	**låg**	**lägre**	**lägst**	low, lower, lowest
	lång	**längre**	**längst**	long, longer, longest
	trång	**trängre**	**trängst**	narrow, narrower, narrowest
	få	**färre**	–	few, fewer
Ψ → Y:	**ung**	**yngre**	**yngst**	young, younger, youngest
	tung	**tyngre**	**tyngst**	heavy, heavier, heaviest
Ö:	**hög**	**högre**	**högst**	high, higher, highest

4.5.3 Irregular comparison

There is a small group of adjectives which compares by adopting a different stem:

Positive	Comparative	Superlative	
god/bra	**bättre**	**bäst**	good, better, best
dålig	**sämre**	**sämst**	bad, worse, worst
dålig/ond	**värre**	**värst**	bad, worse, worst
gammal	**äldre**	**äldst**	old, older, oldest
liten	**mindre**	**minst**	small, smaller, smallest
många	**fler(a)**	**flest**	many, more, most
mycket	**mer(a)**	**mest**	much, more, most

4.5.4 | *Comparison with* **mer, mest**

A large and varied group of adjectives compares using the adverbs **mer** and **mest** rather than an ending. This group includes:

1 Most past participles:

Positive	Comparative	Superlative
komplicerad	***mer* komplicerad**	***mest* komplicerad**
complicated	more complicated	most complicated
ansträngd	***mer* ansträngd**	***mest* ansträngd**
strained	more strained	most strained

Exceptions: Past participles ending in **-en** often add an inflexional ending:

frusen	**frus*nare***	**frus*nast***
cold (lit. frozen)	colder	coldest

2 All present participles:

omfattande	***mer* omfattande**	***mest* omfattande**
wide-ranging	more wide-ranging	most wide-ranging

3 All adjectives of two or more syllables ending in **-isk**:

fantastisk	***mer* fantastisk**	***mest* fantastisk**
fantastic	more fantastic	most fantastic

Notice that all adjectives compared using **mer** and **mest** also inflect according to the indefinite and definite declensions (see 4.5.6):

ett mera typiskt exempel
a more typical example

den mest fantastisk*a* matchen
the most fantastic match

There is an increasing tendency to use **mer, mest** as an alternative to inflectional comparisons:

Det är mest troligt att han avgår.
It's most likely that he will resign.

4.5.5 *Comparison (indefinite) – summary chart*

	Positive	Comparative	Superlative	

1 Comparative with **-are, -ast**. See 4.5.1.

	Positive	Comparative	Superlative	
	glad	**gladare**	**gladast**	happy
	rolig	**roligare**	**roligast**	funny
Notice:	**mager**	**magrare**	**magrast**	thin

2 Comparative with (vowel change and) **-re, -st**. See 4.5.2.

stor	**större**	**störst**	big
lång	**längre**	**längst**	long
ung	**yngre**	**yngst**	young

But notice also

hög	**högre**	**högst**	high

3 Irregular comparison – new stem. See 4.5.3. For use, see 4.5.7.

god/bra	**bättre**	**bäst**	good
dålig	**sämre**	**sämst**	bad
dålig/ond	**värre**	**värst**	bad
gammal	**äldre**	**äldst**	old
liten	**mindre**	**minst**	little
många	**fler(a)**	**flest**	many
mycket	**mer(a)**	**mest**	much

4 Comparison with **mer, mest**. See 4.5.4.

All present and past participles and adjectives with suffixes in **-isk, -ad, -ande**:

typisk	**mer typisk**	**mest typisk**	typical
befogad	**mer befogad**	**mest befogad**	justified
glädjande	**mer glädjande**	**mest glädjande**	pleasing

4.5.6 | Comparison (indefinite and definite)

1 The comparative (when formed with -(a)re (see 4.5.1 ff)) is indeclinable:

Non-neuter	Neuter	Plural
Indefinite		
en vackrare flicka	**ett större hus**	**vackrare flickor/ större hus**
a prettier girl	a bigger house	prettier girls/ bigger houses
Definite		
den vackrare flickan	**det större huset**	**de vackrare flickorna/större husen**
the prettier girl	the bigger house	the prettier girls/ bigger houses

2 The superlative (when formed with -(a)st (see 4.5.1 ff)) inflects in the definite form when used attributively, but does not inflect when used predicatively:

Non-neuter	Neuter	Plural
Predicative		
flickan är vackrast⊗	**huset är nyast⊗**	**bilarna är dyrast⊗**
the girl is prettiest	the house is newest	the cars are dearest
flickan är äldst⊗	**slottet är äldst⊗**	**flickorna är äldst⊗ /slotten är äldst⊗**
the girl is oldest	the castle is oldest	the girls/castles are oldest
kungen är mest älskad⊗		
the king is most beloved		
Attributive		
den vackraste flickan	**det nyaste huset**	**de dyraste bilarna**
the prettiest girl	the newest house	the dearest cars
den äldsta flickan	**det äldsta slottet**	**de äldsta flickorna/ slotten**
the oldest girl	the oldest castle	the oldest girls/castles
den mest älskade kungen		
the most beloved king		

4.5.7 *Use of comparatives and superlatives*

1 god, bra:

Godare, godast = more/most pleasant-tasting.

Bättre and bäst are used in a general sense.

den godaste middagen	the best dinner
Cf. **den bästa uppsatsen**	the best essay

2 dålig:

Värre, värst = more/most of a bad property:

den värsta lögn jag har hört   the worst lie I have heard

Sämre, sämst = less/least of a good property, i.e. poorer/poorest:

byxor av sämre kvalitet   trousers of poorer quality

3 mer, mest/fler, flest = more, most

Mer(a), mest are only used with non-count nouns, while fler(a) and flest are only used with count nouns:

Vill du ha mer kaffe?	Would you like more coffee?
De flesta svenskar gillar sill.	Most Swedes like pickled herring.

If a comparison is implied when using **de flesta,** the noun following takes the end article:

Vem fick de flesta rösterna?   Who received most votes?

4 Absolute comparative (i.e. the comparative element is lost, the adjective indicates a high degree):

Han har vunnit en större summa. (= en ganska stor summa)
He has won a fairly large sum.

Cf. relative comparative:

Summan var större än han trodde.
The sum was larger than he thought.

Notice: **flera** = several (cf. 3 above):

Jag har varit här flera gånger.   I have been here several times.

5 Absolute superlative (i.e. the comparative element is lost, the adjective indicates a very high degree):

De var de bästa vänner.   They were the best of friends.
(mycket goda vänner)

Cf. relative superlative:

De bästa vännerna i vår klass var Per och Ulf.
The best friends in our class were Per and Ulf.

Chapter 5

Pronouns

5.1 Personal and reflexive pronouns – form

Subject pronouns		Object pronouns		Reflexive pronouns	
Singular					
1 **jag**	I	**mig**	me	**mig (mej)**	me/myself
2 **du**	you	**dig**	you	**dig (dej)**	you/yourself
ni	you	**er**	you	**er**	you (see 5.2 (1) below)
3 **han**	he	**honom**	him	**sig (sej)**	him/himself
hon	she	**henne**	her	**sig (sej)**	her/herself
den	it	**den**	it	**sig (sej)**	it/itself
det	it	**det**	it	**sig (sej)**	it/itself
Plural					
1 **vi**	we	**oss**	us	**oss**	we/ourselves
2 **ni**	you	**er**	you	**er**	you/yourselves
3 **de (dom)**	they	**dem (dom)**	them	**sig (sej)**	them/themselves

Notes:
1 Unlike English 'I', **jag** does not have a capital letter except at the beginning of a sentence. **Jag** is pronounced [ja] unless stressed.
2 **Du/ni**, **dig/er**, etc., occasionally have initial capital letters in official communications.
3. Both **de** and **dem** are pronounced [dɔm] except in liturgical and formal language. The written form **dom** is accepted in personal letters and modern fiction, especially in dialogue, though cultivated Swedish retains **de** and **dem** in writing. This has *not* extended to the use of **dom** as a front article before the adjective: **de rika** [dɔm riːka].
4. In personal letters and modern fiction the spellings **mej**, **dej** and **sej** are occasionally found for **mig**, **dig** and **sig**.
5 **Det** is pronounced [deː].
6. There is no separate disjunctive form of the pronoun in Swedish, but the subject form is used for this purpose: – **Hallå du! – Vem? Jag?** 'Hallo there!', 'Who, me?' (See also **5.2(3)**.)

5.2 Use of personal pronouns

1 du/ni: In the singular most people now use the familiar **du**. Although **ni** is sometimes still used as a polite form of address to people being served in restaurants, shops, airports, etc., to many Swedes **ni** now sounds old-fashioned and stand-offish. (See also 5.7.) Note the following idiomatic expressions:

Du, kan du hjälpa mig?	I say/Hey, can you give me a hand?
Snälla du, hjälp mig!	Will you/Please help me!

2 han/hon: **han** is also used to refer to so-called 'higher animals' irrespective of their true gender.

Vilken björn! Han är enorm.
What a bear! He's enormous.

Hon is used to refer to the clock when telling the time and also to the noun **människa** (human being):

Hur mycket är klockan? Hon är fyra.
What's the time? It's four o'clock.

En människa måste bestämma sig för hur hon vill leva.
A person has to decide how he (or she) wants to live.

3 den/det/de: In addition to serving as personal pronouns, these words may also be used as demonstrative pronouns (see 5.8).

Det also has a number of idiomatic usages:

(a) as a complement of **vara/bli** when the verb is followed by a noun or pronoun, irrespective of gender or number:

Vad var det? Det var en katt/jag.
What was that? It was a cat/me.

Vem är hon? Det är min mamma.
Who's she? She's my mum.

Bröderna Olsson. Det är två fina killar.
The Olsson brothers, they're a couple of fine lads.

(b) as a formal subject (see 12.6.1, 12.7.7):

Det är svårt att lära sig tyska.   It's hard to learn German.

Det finns ingen matta på golvet.
There's no carpet on the floor.

Det bor många svenskar här.
There are a lot of Swedes living here.

Note that Swedish may use **det** + any intransitive verb in this way. English generally uses only the verb 'to be'.

(c) in passive constructions without a real subject (see 7.5.17):

Det skrivs/pratas mycket om henne.
There's a lot written/said about her.

Det hörs att hon inte är svensk.
You can hear she's not Swedish.

(d) as an impersonal subject:

Det blåste och det snöade. It was windy and snowing.

Det kändes mycket kallt. It felt very cold.

Det syns att han är sjuk. You can see he's ill.

Hur står det till? How are you?/How are things going?

Hur gick det? What happened?

(e) as an object of verbs expressing 'think/believe/hope/say', etc. (cf. English 'so'):

Är han död? De fruktar/tror/hoppas/säger det.
Is he dead? They fear/think/hope/say so.

Note also:

Olle var hungrig. Och det var vi också. Olle was hungry. And so were we.

(f) in answer to questions, without an English equivalent, as a complement of **vara/bli** or an object of auxiliary verbs:

Är du rik? Nej, det är jag inte. Are you rich? No, I'm not.

Kan du svenska? Ja, det kan jag. Do you speak Swedish? Yes, I do.

Note also:

Hon ser snäll ut, och det är hon. She looks kind, and she is too.

(g) without an English equivalent when referring back to a whole clause:

Han påstår att han bor i villa, men det gör han inte.
He claims that he lives in a detached house, but he doesn't.

Summary of the major uses of *det*:

Function	Used with	English equivalent
personal pronoun	any verb to refer back to neuter noun in singular	it
demonstrative pronoun	cf. 5.8	that/it/that one
complement of **vara/bli**	**vara/bli** + noun/pronoun	it/he/she/they
formal subject	**vara/bli** + adjective	it
	any intransitive verb	there
	any passive verb	there
impersonal subject	impersonal verb	it
object	verbs expressing say/think/ hope/believe, etc.	so
prepositioned object	cf. 12.7.1	
answering questions	**vara/bli** or auxiliary verb	–
refers back to clause	any verb	–/it/that or infinitive

5.3 Reflexive pronouns

The reflexive pronoun is used when the object of a sentence or clause is also the subject. Reflexive forms are identical to object forms for all but the third person:

Jag **har skurit** *mig.*	I have cut myself.
Stäng dörren efter *dig!*	Close the door behind you.

/*Du*/ is understood as subject in imperatives.

Han **har skurit** *sig.*	He has cut himself.
Han **stängde dörren efter** *sig.*	He closed the door behind him.
De **hade inga pengar på** *sig.*	They had no money on them.

Note that the reflexive forms must be used in Swedish. There is a great deal of difference between **Han sköt honom** (Object, 'He shot him') and **Han sköt sig** (Reflexive, 'He shot himself')!

There is one important and frequent exception to the main rule. After verbs followed by object and infinitive constructions (see 7.5.1 (3)) the reflexive pronoun idiomatically refers to the object, and the personal pronoun to the subject of the main clause:

Han (S) **bad doktorn** (O) **tvätta** *sig* (RP).

He asked the doctor to wash himself.

Han (S) **bad doktorn** (O) **tvätta** *honom* (PP).

He asked the doctor to wash him.

The reflexive pronouns are used with a number of verbs (see 7.5.14) regarded as expressing reflexive actions in Swedish, but where the reflexive idea is absent in English:

gifta sig (get married), **raka sig** (have a shave)

5.4 *Själv*

Själv (-t, -a) is only used for emphasis. It is not itself reflexive (cf. 5.3 above):

Jag kan göra det själv.	I can do it myself.
Killarna själva målade huset.	The boys painted the house themselves.
Han älskar bara sig själv.	He only loves himself.

5.5 Possessive pronouns

In Swedish the possessive pronoun and possessive adjective have the same form:

Boken är min.	The book is mine.
Det är min bok.	It is my book.

First and second person possessives agree with the noun:

Det är *din* hatt, *ditt* paraply och *dina* stövlar.

Third person possessives ending in -s do not inflect:

Det är *hans* hatt, *hans* paraply och *hans* stövlar.

Reflexive possessives are given in brackets in the following table. These forms are explained more fully in 5.6.

		Non-neuter	Neuter	Plural	
Singular					
I		min	mitt	mina	my, mine
2	familiar	din	ditt	dina	your, yours
	formal	er	ert	era	
3		hans	hans	hans	his
		sin	sitt	sina	(see 5.6)
		hennes	hennes	hennes	her, hers
		sin	sitt	sina	(see 5.6)
		dess	dess	dess	its
		sin	sitt	sina	(see 5.6)
Plural					
I		vår	vårt	våra	our, ours
2		er	ert	era	your, yours
3		deras	deras	deras	their, theirs
		sin	sitt	sina	(see 5.6)

Notes:

I Possessive pronouns have no genitive form:

min brors böcker my brother's books

2 Noun + 'of' before a possessive pronoun in English is usually rendered in Swedish by **till** and object pronoun (see 10.3.5 (1c)):

a friend of mine **en vän till mig**

3 The possessive pronoun **dess** is reserved almost exclusively for formal written Swedish. The definite article is often used as a Swedish equivalent to 'its':

Vättern och dess omgivningar. Lake Vättern and its surroundings.
Bilen tappade ett av hjulen. The car lost one of its wheels.
Filmen minns jag men inte titeln. I recall the film but not its title.

4 English possessive adjectives with parts of the body, clothing, etc., are generally rendered by the Swedish definite article if there is no doubt as to ownership:

Aj! Jag har stukat foten. Ouch! I've twisted my ankle.
Ta av er skorna! Take off your shoes!
Han har tappat minnet. He has lost his memory.

5. In spoken Swedish the possessive pronouns for the first and second persons plural have colloquial forms **våran/vårat, er/erat** which exist alongside the standard written forms. See 1.2.10 (2), Note 5.

5.6 Non-reflexive and reflexive possessives: *hans* or *sin*?

1 The reflexive possessives **sin/sitt/sina** (inflected according to the gender/number of the noun qualified) refer to possession by the third person subject (noun, personal, interrogative, or indefinite pronoun) of the clause:

> He loves his wife, his child and his parents.
> **Han** älskar *sin* fru, *sitt* barn och *sina* föräldrar.
> S ←———————|——————|————————|

Sin/sitt/sina cannot be used to qualify the subject of the clause:

> His wife loves him.   **Hans fru älskar honom.**
> S

2 The non-reflexive forms do not refer back to the subject of the clause:

> Olle is cross. Why? Because Åke went out with his wife.
> **Olle är sur. Varför det? Därför att Åke gick ut med hans fru.**
> S   S   O

The non-reflexive possessive pronouns **hans, hennes, dess, deras** (indeclinable) may qualify the subject or object of a clause:

> His wife is a teacher.   I've seen his wife at school.
> **Hans fru är lärare.**   **Jag har sett *hans* fru på skolan.**
> S   O

There are two ways of maintaining a distinction between the areas of usage of these different forms:

(a) Draw an arrow to the 'possessor'. Is the 'possessor' the subject of the clause?

(b) Can you insert the word 'own' before the object in English? If so, use a form of **sin/sitt/sina**. If not, then use a non-reflexive form.

3 A problem arises when there is more than one clause in the sentence:

> They think that their teacher is boring.
> S   /SC S

Here 'their teacher' is the subject of the subordinate clause and 'their' does not refer back, but qualifies the subject. Therefore use **deras**.

> **De tycker att deras lärare är tråkig.**
> S   /SC S

4 A confusing case occurs when the possessive precedes the subject:

Despite his appearance he was very young.

Trots *sitt* utseende var *han* mycket ung.

←————————————S

5 In clauses with ellipsis (object + infinitive), when there is no finite verb
in the clause, **sin/sitt/sina** may refer to the *implied subject* of the clause:

I heard her call her husband.　**Jag hörde *henne* ropa på *sin* man.**
S　　IS　　O　　　　　　　S　　　　　　IS ←————————

I saw him kick his dog.　　　**Jag såg *honom* sparka *sin* hund.**
S　IS　　O　　　　　　　　　　S　　　　IS ←————————

To test this, expand the ellipted clause into a full clause and apply the
basic rules (see 1, 2 above):

Jag såg att *han* sparkade *sin* hund.
S　　/SC S ←————————O

6 Note the idiomatic use of **sin/sitt/sina** in such phrases as:

Det är inte lätt att älska sin nästa.
Loving your neighbour is not easy.

Att offra sin hälsa på cigaretter är dumt.
It's stupid to sacrifice your health for cigarettes.

7 Note the idiomatic use of **sin/sitt/sina** in abbreviated comparisons:

Han är längre än sin fru.　　He is taller than his wife.

cf.
Han är längre än hans fru är.　He is taller than his wife is.

8 Note the use of **sin/sitt/sina** in expressions with **var sin** etc.:

Vi fick var sin banan.　　We got a banana each.

Flickorna fick var sitt äpple.　The girls got an apple each.

Notice that **var** is indeclinable in such phrases, and that the choice of
sin/sitt/sina is determined by the gender/number of the noun qualified.

Forms of address

For personal pronouns see 5.1 f.

1 By far the most common forms of address in modern Swedish are **du** (you, singular) and **ni** (you, plural). From the 1960s onwards, as old class barriers became less marked, **du** became almost universally accepted in Sweden. There are, however, a number of alternative conventions.

2 Formal or polite **ni** is still used occasionally for both singular and plural 'you' in more conservative circles, amongst older people who are not on first-name terms, and (with a capital letter: see 14.1 (5)) in formal business and official communications.

3 Titles: Previously a title and a third person construction were sometimes used to convey formal deference when addressing someone. (English has a similar construction. Cf: 'Would madam like to try on the coat?' and **Skulle damen vilja prova kappan?**) Unless used ironically, this form of address is reserved only for very formal occasions in modern Swedish.

> **Har kungen några önskemål?**
> Do you have any wishes, Your Majesty?

4 Impersonal constructions: Especially when asking a question, impersonal constructions provide a very neutral – but by no means unfriendly or impolite – form of address between people not personally acquainted.

> **Vad får det lov att vara?**   Can I help you? (in a shop)
> **Hur var namnet?**   What is your name?
> **Önskas socker?**   Do you take/Would you like sugar?

5 **Man** is used:

(a) as an alternative to **du** as a slightly ironic form of address:

> **Har man sovit bättre i natt?**   Did you sleep better last night?

(b) as an equivalent to English 'one' or 'you':

> **Man kan aldrig veta.**   You never know/One never knows.

6 Pejorative expressions: Swedish uses the possessive pronoun (5.5) not the personal pronoun in pejorative expressions such as **Din dumbom!** (You fool!), **Era idioter** (You idiots!), and also in **Din stackare!** (You poor thing!).

5.8   Demonstrative pronouns

Non-neuter	Neuter	Plural
den **flickan**	*det* **huset**	*de* **flickorna/husen**
this/that girl	this/that house	these/those girls/houses
den här **flickan**	*det här* **huset**	*de här* **flickorna/husen**
this girl	this house	these girls/houses
den där **flickan**	*det där* **huset**	*de där* **flickorna/husen**
that girl	that house	those girls/houses
denna **flicka**⊗	*detta* **hus**⊗	*dessa* **flickor**⊗**/hus**
this/that girl	this/that house	these/these girls/houses
samma **flicka**⊗	*samma* **hus**⊗	*samma* **flickor**⊗**/hus**⊗
the same girl	the same house	the same girls/houses
en sådan **flicka**⊗	*ett sådant* **hus**⊗	*sådana* **flickor**⊗**/hus**⊗
such a girl	such a house	such girls/houses

Notes:

1 **Den** etc. (always stressed when used as a demonstrative pronoun) is preferred with abstract nouns:

> **Det året kom vi till Sverige.**   That year we arrived in Sweden.

2 **Den här**, **den där**, etc., are found in both speech and writing, and require an end article on the noun.

3 **Denna**, **detta**, etc., are generally reserved for written Swedish and require no end article on the noun.

4 As in English, demonstratives may be used predicatively (i.e. independently of a noun). They then take the number/gender of the noun to which they refer:

> **De här tavlorna är dyrare än**   These pictures are more expensive than
> **de där.**   those.
> **Detta är något nytt.**   This is something new.

There is no equivalent in Swedish to English 'one' in phrases like 'this one/that one', etc:

> **Jag tar det här, inte det där.**   I'll take this one, not that one.

Note that the demonstrative **de** (these, those) has an object form when used predicatively:

> **Jag tar de här skorna, inte dem.**   I'll take these shoes, not those.

5 **Samma** is only used attributively; **densamma**, etc., is used predicatively and in more formal Swedish. There is neither front nor end article with **samma**.

> **Vi ses nästa vecka. Samma tid,**   See you next week. Same time, same
> **samma plats.**   place.
> **Hon är alltid densamma.**   She's always the same.

6 **Sådan** is preceded by the singular indefinite article, not followed by it as in English. In colloquial Swedish it is combined with **här/där**:

> **en sådan (här) flicka**   such a girl/a girl like this

Notice:

> **Jag tar fem sådana.**   I will have five of those.
> **En sådan stor bil han har!**   What a big car he has!

5.9 **Determinative pronouns**

Non-neuter	Neuter	Plural
den flicka⊗ som	*det* hus⊗ som	*de* flickor⊗/hus⊗ som

1 The determinative is a kind of demonstrative that directs attention to a following relative clause. When the determinative qualifies a noun, the noun has *no* end article (cf. demonstratives 5.8 above):

Cf. Demonstrative:

> *De turisterna* **därborta fick mycket sol.**
> Those tourists over there got a lot of sun.

Determinative:

> *De turister som* **åkte till Island fick mycket sol, medan** *de turister som* **åkte till Italien fick regn varje dag.**
> Those/The tourists who went to Iceland got a lot of sun, whilst those/the tourists who went to Italy had rain every day.

2 Determinatives are used when the following relative clause is essential to the sentence ('restrictive clause'). Notice that a contrast is often implied. If the relative clause is merely an afterthought and may be deleted ('non-restrictive clause'), then an end article is used. Cf.

> **De fabriker som anställer ungdomar bör hjälpas.** (restrictive)
> (Only) those firms employing young people should be helped.

> **Fabrikerna, som anställer ungdomar, bör hjälpas.**
> The firms, which employ young people, should be helped.

3 When the determinative is used without a noun **de som** is now accepted as an object form for **dem som**:

> **Jag kände ingen av de som/dem som var där.**
> I knew none of those who were there.

> **Samhället straffar de som/dem som bryter mot lagen.**
> Society punishes those who break the law.

5.10 Relative pronouns

Relative pronouns introduce a subordinate (relative) clause, referring back to a correlative in the main clause:

Han är *en vän*   som man kan lita på.
        correlative ⌋
He is a friend   whom one can rely on.

Relative pronouns include:

som	the most frequent relative pronoun	which, who, what, that
vars	genitive of **som,** sing. and plural (written Swedish)	whose
vilkas	genitive of **som,** plural only (written Swedish)	whose
vilken n-n.		
vilket n. = **som**		who, which, what, that
vilka pl.		
vad		what

Examples of use:

Ser du *pojken* som leker därborta?
Do you see the boy who is playing over there?

Mannen, vars dotter ska gifta sig, är sjuk.
The man whose daughter is getting married is ill.

Föräldrarna, vars/vilkas dotter ska gifta sig, är sjuka.
The parents whose daughter is getting married are ill.

Det är *allt*, vad jag vet.
That's all that I know.

Notes:

1 **Vilken,** etc., is rarely used other than in formal Swedish. Note, however, that **vilket** (*not* **som**) must be used to refer back to a whole clause:

Hon har börjat studera, vilket gläder mig.
She's started studying, which pleases me.

2 **Som** may be omitted when it does not serve as a subject in a subordinate clause:

Han är den intelligentaste student (som) jag har träffat.
        O   S
He's the most intelligent student (that) I've met.

But:

Ser du pojken som står därborta?
　　　　　　　　S

Can you see the boy (who is) standing over there?

3 In contrast to English, a preposition does not appear in the same clause directly before **som**:

Den man som du pratar om ...　　The man of whom you are speaking
　　　　　　　　　　　　　　　　The man that you are speaking of ...

4 When used as the subject of a relative clause **vad** is followed by **som** (see 5.11 (4)):

Vi vet inte vad som hände honom.　We don't know what happened to him.
　　　　　　　　S

5.11　Interrogative pronouns (*v*-words)

Interrogative pronouns introduce a direct or indirect question.

Interrogative pronouns (v-words) include:

vem, vilka	who (sg.), who (pl.)
vad [vɑːd] or [va]	what
vad ... för något/någonting	what (spoken Swedish)
vilken n-n., **vilket** n., **vilka** pl.	which
när	when
var	where
hur	how
varför	why

Notes:

1 When rendering English 'who' remember that **vem** is only used in the singular, **vilka** is only used in the plural:

Vem var det som ringde?　　　　Who was it that phoned?
Vilka är det som kommer ikväll?　Who are coming tonight?

2 'What kind of' is often rendered in spoken Swedish by **vad för en/ett** + singular noun or **vad för** + plural noun:

Vad köpte du för (en) bil?　　　What kind of car did you buy?
Vad köpte du för (ett) hus?　　What kind of house did you buy?
Vad köpte du för böcker?　　　What kind of books did you buy?

3 **Vilken** etc. may be used attributively and predicatively:

Vilka dikter har du redan läst?　Which poems have you already read?
Vilken vill du läsa nu?　　　　Which (one) do you want to read now?

4 Notice that **som** is inserted after **vad**, **vilken** etc. + noun when this is the subject of a subordinate clause (indirect question):

Jag undrar *vad* **(O)** *han* **(S) gör.**	I wonder what he's doing.
Jag undrar *vad* **(O)** *som* **(S) händer.**	I wonder what's happening.
Jag undrar *vem som* **(S) kommer.**	I wonder who's coming.
Jag undrar *vilka böcker* **(S)** *som* **är dina.**	I wonder which books are yours.

5 Notice the use of **vilken**, etc., in exclamations:

Vilken härlig dag!	What a lovely day!
Vilket hemskt väder!	What awful weather!

6 Notice other interrogatives using **hur**: **hur länge?** (how long?); **hur långt?** (how far?); **hur mycket?** (how much?); **hur många** (how many?); **hur dags?** (what time?).

5.12 Indefinite pronouns

Indefinite pronouns include:

Non-neuter	Neuter	Plural	
någon	**något**	**några**	some, any, someone, anything
ingen	**inget**	**inga**	no, none, no-one, nothing
all	**allt**	**alla**	all, everything
varje	**varje**		each, every
varenda	**vartenda**		each and every
var	**vart**		each, every
var och en	**vart och ett**		each and every one
varannan	**vartannat**	**varandra**	every other, each other
vem som	**vad som**	**vilka som**	anyone at all,
helst	**helst**	**helst**	anything at all
man			one, you
Possessive form of **man**:		**ens**	one's
Object form of **man**:		**en**	one, you
Reflexive form of **man**:		**sig**	oneself (see 5.3)
Reflexive possessive form of **man**:		**sin**	one's own (see 5.6)
Note also the pronominal adverbs:			
någonsin			sometime, ever
någonstans			somewhere

Notes:

1 (a) **Ingen** etc./**inte någon**, etc., are alternatives as object in a main clause with simple tense (present, past):

    De (S) **såg** *ingen/inte någon* (O) **i skogen.**   They saw no-one in the forest.

(b) **Inte någon**, etc., must be used as the object in a main clause with complex tense (perfect, pluperfect, modal + main verb) or in a subordinate clause. When **inte någon** constructions are found in the subordinate clause, **inte** precedes the finite verb (see also 12.7.5):

    Jag har *inte* **sett** *någon* (O) **i skogen.**   I haven't seen anyone in the forest.

    Jag kan *inte* **se** *någon* (O).   I can't see anyone.

    De sa, att de *inte* **hade sett** *någon* (O) **i skogen.**
    They said that they hadn't seen anyone in the forest.

2 (a) **All**, etc., may be used with or without a definite article on the noun following in much the same way as in English:

    Alla böcker är dyra.   All books are expensive.

    Alla böckerna hade sålts.   All the books had been sold.

(b) English 'all' = 'the whole (of)' is usually rendered by **hela** + the noun with end article singular:

    Har du läst hela boken?   Have you read all (of) the book?

(c) **Allt** corresponds to 'everything'; **alla** corresponds to 'everyone':

    Han säljer allt till alla.   He sells everything to everyone.

3 **Varje** (indeclinable), and **var/vart** are synonymous but not always interchangeable:

(a) **Varje** is common in spoken Swedish, and is used pronominally only after a preposition:

    Fem påsar med 12 kg i varje.   Five bags with 12 kilos in each.

    Varje påse innehåller 12 kg.   Each (bag) holds 12 kilos.

(b) **Var/vart** is preferred before ordinals:

    Han kommer var tredje vecka.
    He comes every third week/every three weeks.

4 **Varenda/vartenda** and **var och en/vart och ett** are more emphatic than **varje/var**.

(a) **Varenda** is used attributively before the indefinite form of the noun:

    Vartenda fel ska rättas.   Every single error must be corrected.

(b) **Var och en** is often followed by **av** + plural noun or pronoun:

    Var och en (av oss) gick hem till sig. Each one (of us) went home.

    Var och en av bilarna var rostig.   Every single one of the cars was rusty.

5 **Varandra** is restricted in meaning to 'one another/each other':

    Vi känner inte varandra.   We don't know each other.

6 (a) **Man** is used far more commonly in Swedish than the rather stilted English 'one'. It occasionally replaces **jag**. Note the form **en** is used as an object or after prepositions:

    Man vet aldrig vad som kan hända en.
    You never know what might happen to you.

(b) The possessive forms **ens** and **sin/sitt/sina** are non-reflexive and reflexive respectively (cf. 5.6):

    Ens ord kan missförstås.   One's words may be misunderstood.

    Man måste göra sin plikt.   One must do one's duty.

Chapter 6

Numerals

6.1 Cardinal and ordinal numbers

	Cardinal numbers	Ordinal numbers
0	noll	
1	ett/en	första
2	två	andra
3	tre	tredje
4	fyra	fjärde
5	fem	femte
6	sex	sjätte
7	sju	sjunde
8	åtta	åttonde
9	nio [ni:ɷ] or [ni:ə]	nionde
10	tio [ti:ɷ] or [ti:ə]	tionde
11	elva	elfte
12	tolv	tolfte
13	tretton	trettonde
14	fjorton [fjɷ:tɔn]	fjortonde
15	femton	femtonde
16	sexton	sextonde
17	sjutton	sjuttonde
18	arton	artonde

19	nitton	nittonde
20	**tjugo** [ɕʉːgω], [ɕʉːgu] or [ɕʉːgi]	**tjugonde**
21	**tjugoett/tjugoen**	**tjugoförsta**
22	**tjugotvå**	**tjugoandra**
30	**tretti(o)**	**trettionde**
40	**fyrti(o)** [føti]	**fyrtionde**
50	**femti(o)**	**femtionde**
60	**sexti(o)**	**sextionde**
70	**sjutti(o)**	**sjuttionde**
80	**åtti(o)**	**åttionde**
90	**nitti(o)**	**nittionde**
100	**(ett) hundra**	**hundrade**
101	**(ett) hundraett (-en)**	**hundraförsta**
1 000	**(ett) tusen**	**tusende**
1 001	**(ett) tusenett (-en)**	**tusenförsta**
1 000 000	**en miljon**	**miljonte**
1 000 000 000	**en miljard**	

Notes:

1 **Miljon, miljard** have plurals in **-er**.

2 The suffix **-en** is generally used before both neuter and non-neuter nouns: **tjugoen bilar** cf. **tjugoen hus**, *But:* **tjugoett/trettioett**, etc., are used with a small number of neuter nouns signifying, for example, years, numbers, currency values and clock times: **fyrtioett år**, **nummer femtioett**, **tre (och) fyrtioett på eftermiddagen**.

3 Unlike English, spoken Swedish has no 'and' between thousands/hundreds and tens (see also 6.2 (6)): 423 = **fyrahundratjugotre** = four hundred *and* twenty-three.

6.2 Major uses of cardinal and ordinal numbers

1 Cardinal numbers have a special form that may be used as a noun.

(a) **En etta, en tvåa, en trea** etc.:
  (i) The number itself, position in a race: **Hon kom tvåa.**
  (ii) Bus, tram number: **Ta femman till stationen.**
  (iii) Size of flat (number of rooms): **De har en trea i Åby.**
  (iv) Size of clothes, shoes: **Fyrtiettorna passar bäst.**

(b)

en femma	a five-kronor coin
en tia	a ten-kronor coin

2 Ordinal numbers

(a) Ordinal numbers (indeclinable in form) are frequently found after the front article, possessive adjective or noun in the genitive:

Det är den första idag.	It's the first (day of the month) today.
Det här är Olles tredje bil.	This is Olle's third car.
Vårt andra barn heter Viola.	Our second child is called Viola.

(b) **1:a, 2:a, 3:e**, etc., are common abbreviations for **första, andra, tredje**, etc. In Swedish the number alone is often sufficient to indicate an ordinal:

måndagen 4 juni	= **måndagen den fjärde juni**
3 pers. sing.	= **tredje person singularis**

3 Fractions

Fractions are largely formed from ordinal numbers by adding **-del**:

¼ = **en fjärdedel**, ⅗ = **tre femtedelar**, etc.

Note that the **-de** of ordinals ending in **-onde** is assimilated in fractions:

⅛	**en åttondel**
⅒	**en tiondel**, etc.
1½	**en och en halv/halvannan** – (e.g. **halvannan timme**)
	ett och ett halvt/halvtannat – (e.g. **halvtannat år**)
2½	**två och en halv**
¼	**en fjärdedel**
⅔	**två tredjedelar**
⅕	**en femtedel**
⅑	**en niondel**

Half = **halv** (-t, -a), i.e. an adjective which inflects:

en halv sida (NB: word order)
half a page

halva sidan
half the page

ett halvt äpple
half an apple

fem och ett halvt år (NB: sing.)
five and a half years

två och ett halvt äpple (NB: sing.)
two and a half apples

halv två
half past one (see 6.3)

Half = **hälft -en, er** i.e. a noun which inflects:

första hälften av filmen
the first half of the film

hälften så stor som i fjor
half as big as last year

4 Decimals

3,5	**tre komma fem**	3.5 (NB: three point five)
3 000	**tretusen**	3,000
3 000 000	**tre miljoner**	3,000,000

5 **-tal**: Neuter nouns may be formed by adding **-tal** (also **-tals**) to cardinal numbers to render:

(a) an approximate number:

Han skrev ett hundratal brev.
He wrote a hundred or so letters.

Tusentals sjöfåglar dödades.
Thousands of seabirds were killed.

(b) a decade or century:

en författare från 1900-talet
an author from the 20th century

EU på 90-talet
the EU in the (19)90s

6 Dates

(a) Years are usually given in figures, but if written out in full are written as one word. The word **hundra** is not omitted in spoken or written Swedish and there is no **och** between the hundreds and tens:

1984	**nittonhundraåttifyra**
2007	**tjugohundrasju**

(b) The English preposition 'in' before years has no equivalent in Swedish (see 10.3.2):

Han är född (år) 1944.
He was born in 1944.

(c) Days of the month: see 2(b) above.

7 Telephone numbers. The digits after the regional/mobile dialling code are frequently given in pairs: thus 0709-12 34 56 is spoken as '**noll sju noll nio – tolv trettifyra femtisex**'.

8 Temperature

– 5°C **Det är fem grader kallt** or **Det är minus fem grader.**

+ 15°C Det är femton grader (varmt) or **Det är plus femton (grader).**

9 Money

3:00 **tre kronor**

103:50 etthundratre och femti/etthundratre kronor och femti öre

6.3 **Time by the clock**

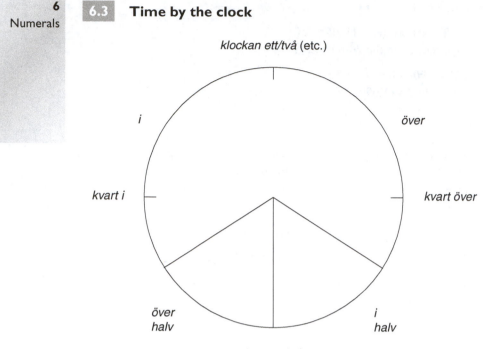

klockan ett/två (etc.)

i

över

kvart i

kvart över

över
halv

i
halv

halv ett/två

1 What is the time? etc.

Hur mycket är klockan? **Vad är klockan?**	What time is it?
Klockan/Hon är ett.	The time/It is one o'clock.
Klockan är en minut över/i ett.	It is one minute past/to one.
Klockan är fem (minuter) över tre.	It is five (minutes) past three.
Klockan är (en) kvart över fyra.	It is (a) quarter past four.
Klockan är fem (minuter) i halv sex.	It is 25 past five.
Klockan är halv sex.	It is half past five.
Klockan är fem (minuter) över halv sex.	It is 25 (minutes) to six.

2 'What time . . .?' etc.

Hur dags/När går tåget?	What time/When does the train leave?

Klockan tre.	At three o'clock.	Time by the clock
Klockan fem och fyrtifem.	At five forty-five.	
Klockan kvart i sex.	At a quarter to six.	
kl. 05.45 = (noll) fem fyrtifem	(At) 05.45 (in timetables etc.)	

Notes:

1 'Half past' an hour in English is always expressed as 'half (to)' the next hour in Swedish:

halv fem	half past four
halv ett	half past twelve

2 Swedes have a special way of expressing time in the period between 21 minutes past the hour and 21 minutes to the hour (see clock diagram):

sex minuter i halv fyra	3.24
tre minuter över halv två	1.33

3 The word **minuter** is often omitted, but as a general rule it is best retained.

Chapter 7

Verbs

7.1   Verb forms in outline

In modern Swedish there is only one form of the verb for all persons, singular and plural, in each of the various tenses of the verb (cf., however, 7.2.7 Note 2).

Swedish has no continuous form of the verb (cf. 7.5.5 (3)) but, like English, employs auxiliary verbs to help form the future, perfect and pluperfect tenses (7.5.7 ff).

For learning purposes it is a convenient simplification to consider the formation of the tenses as the addition of an ending to the basic part of the verb – the *stem* (see below).

There are four principal types or conjugations of Swedish verbs. Conjugations I, II and III are *weak* conjugations, forming the past tense by the addition of an ending. All their forms can be built up simply on the basis of their infinitive/present forms. Conjugation IV is *strong*, forming its past tense by changing the stem vowel. The table summarizes generalized endings for each conjugation and tense:

Conjugation	Imperative = stem	Infinitive = stem + *a*/⊗	Present = stem + er/r	
I	**arbeta**	**arbeta**	**arbetar**	work
IIa	**ring**	**ringa**	**ringer**	ring
IIb	**köp**	**köpa**	**köper**	buy
III	**sy**	**sy**	**syr**	sew
IV	**bit**	**bita**	**biter**	bite
	bjud	**bjuda**	**bjuder**	invite

Conjugation	Past stem + *de/te/dde*	Supine stem + *t/tt*
I	**arbetade**	**arbetat**
IIa	**ringde**	**ringt**
IIb	**köpte**	**köpt**
III	**sydde**	**sytt**
IV	stem with *vowel change*	stem with *vowel change* + **it**
	drack	**druckit**
	bjöd	**bjudit**

Conjugation	Present participle stem + *(a)nde/ende*	Past participle stem + *d/t/dd/en*
I	**arbetande**	**arbetad**
IIa	**ringande**	**ringd**
IIb	**köpande**	**köpt**
III	**syende**	**sydd**
IV	**bitande**	**biten**
	bjudande	**bjuden**

7.2 The four conjugations

7.2.1 First conjugation

Infinitive + ⊗	Present +*r*	Past +*de*	Supine +*t*	Past participle +*d*	
arbeta	**arbetar**	**arbetade**	**arbetat**	**arbetad**	work
studera	**studerar**	**studerade**	**studerat**	**studerad**	study

Includes: two-thirds of all verbs (a quarter of all active verbs) and all new verbs, e.g. **dejta** (date), **jobba** (work), **parkera** (park), **surfa** (surf).

Some very frequent conjugation I verbs are:

berätta (tell), **bruka** (use), **börja** (begin), **fråga** (ask), **förklara** (explain), **handla** (shop), **kalla** (call), **kosta** (cost), **lämna** (leave), **mena** (think, mean), **spela** (play), **svara** (answer), **tala** (speak), **verka** (seem), **visa** (show), **öka** (increase), **öppna** (open).

7.2.2 | Irregular verbs of the first conjugation

Irregular forms are marked *. Forms within brackets ( ) are less common.

Infinitive	Present	Past	Supine	Past participle	
besluta	**beslutar/ besluter**	**beslutade/ beslöt**	**beslutat/ beslutit**	**beslutad/ besluten**	decide
betala	**betalar**	**betalade**	**betalt*** **(betalat)**	**betald*** **(betalad)**	pay
koka	**kokar/**	**kokade/ (kokte***	**kokat/ kokt***	**kokad/ kokt*)**	boil

7.2.3 | Second conjugation

The second conjugation is divided into two types:

IIa – stem in voiced consonant, past tense in **-de**

IIb – stem in voiceless consonant (i.e. **-k/-p/-s/-t/-x**) or in **-n**, past tense in **-te**

IIa

Infinitive +*a*	Present +*er*	Past +*de*	Supine +*t*	Past participle +*d*	
följa	**följer**	**följde**	**följt**	**följd**	follow
bygga	**bygger**	**byggde**	**byggt**	**byggd**	build

The following patterns vary slightly from the main paradigm:

1 Stem in -r. No ending in present tense:

köra   **kör⊗**   **körde**   **kört**   **körd**   drive

Like **köra**: **lära** (learn), **höra** (hear), **röra** (move), **störa** (disturb), **begära** (demand), **föra** (lead), **hyra** (rent).

2 Stem in *vowel* + **d**. Doubling of -**d** in past tense and past participle but lose the -**d** and double the -**t** in the supine:

betyda   **betyder**   **betydde**   **betytt**   **betydd**   mean

Like **betyda**: **föda** (feed/bear), **träda** (step), **antyda** (hint), **lyda** (obey).

3 Stem in *consonant* + **d**. Add only -**e** in past tense and drop the -**d** in the supine. In the past participle no extra -**d** is added:

använda   **använder**   **använde**   **använt**   **använd**   use

Like **använda**: **tända** (light), **sända** (send), **hända** (happen).

4 Stem in -**l**. No ending in present tense:

tåla   **tål⊗**   **tålde**   **tålt**   **tåld**   tolerate

Like **tåla**: **mala** (grind).

5 Stem in -**mm**. Single **m** before consonant or in final position. See 14.2:

glömma   **glömmer**   **glömde**   **glömt**   **glömd**   forget

Like **glömma**: **drömma** (dream), **gömma** (hide), **skrämma** (frighten).

6 Stem in -**nn**. Single **n** before consonant. See 14.2:

känna   **känner**   **kände**   **känt**   **känd**   know

Like **känna**: **bränna** (burn), **påminna** (remind).

7 Stem in *mutated vowel* + **j**. Mutation and **j** in infinitive, present tense only:

välja   **väljer**   **valde**   **valt**   **vald**   choose

dölja   **döljer**   **dolde**   **dolt**   **dold**   conceal

Like **välja**: **vänja** (get used to), **svälja** (swallow).

Like **dölja**: **smörja** (lubricate).

8 Infinitive, present only in *mutated vowel*:

böra	**bör**	**borde**	**bort**	–	ought, should

Like **böra**: **töra** (be likely).

IIb

Infinitive +*a*	Present +*er*	Past +*te*	Supine +*t*	Past participle +*t*	
köpa	**köper**	**köpte**	**köpt**	**köpt**	buy
trycka	**trycker**	**tryckte**	**tryckt**	**tryckt**	press

The following patterns vary slightly from the main paradigm:

1 Stem in -*vowel* + **t**. Doubling of final consonant in supine and past participle:

möta	**möter**	**mötte**	**mött**	**mött**	meet

Like **möta**: **byta** (exchange), **mäta** (measure), **sköta** (look after).

2 Stem in -*consonant* + **t**. Add only -e in past tense, no ending in supine and past participle:

gifta	**gifter**	**gifte**	**gift⊗**	**gift⊗**	marry

Like **gifta**: **mista** (lose), **lyfta** (lift), **smälta** (melt), **fästa** (attach).

7.2.4 | *Irregular verbs of the second conjugation*

Irregular forms are marked *. Forms preceded by + exist only in compounds, e.g. **medhavd mat**, food brought along.

Infinitive	Present	Past	Supine	Past participle	
bringa*	bringar*	bragte	bragt	bragt	bring about
glädja	gläder*	gladde*	glatt*	–	please
göra*	gör*	gjorde	gjort	gjord	do, make
ha	har*	hade	haft*	+havd*	have
heta	heter	hette	hetat*	–	be called
kunna	kan*	kunde	kunnat*	–	can, be able
lägga	lägger	la(de)*	lagt*	lagd*	lay (tr.)
–	måste	måste	måst	–	must
skola*	ska(ll)*	skulle	skolat*	–	shall
stödja*	stöder	stödde	stött	stödd	support
säga	säger	sa(de)*	sagt*	sagd*	say
sälja	säljer	sålde*	sålt*	såld*	sell
sätta	sätter	satte*	satt*	satt*	place
(varda)	–	vart*	–	–	become
veta*	vet*	visste	vetat*	–	know
vilja*	vill*	ville	velat*	–	want
växa	växer	växte	växt/vuxit	vuxen*	grow

7.2.5 | Third conjugation

Infinitive -vowel (not a)	Present +r	Past +dde	Supine +tt	Past participle +dd	
sy	syr	sydde	sytt	sydd	sew
bo	bor	bodde	bott	+bodd	live

Includes: most verbs with stems ending in a long stressed vowel other than -a.

The stem vowel is shortened before the past tense ending in -**dde** and supine ending in -**tt**. This is a small and non-productive group. Vowels involved are:

-**e** **ske** (occur), **bete** (behave)
-**o** **tro** (believe), **ro** (row), **bero** (depend)
-**y** **bry** (care), **fly** (flee), **avsky** (hate), **gry** (dawn)
-**ö** **strö** (strew)
-**ä** **klä** (dress)
-**å** **nå** (reach)

Note: Several verbs of this group possess longer forms which are now formal or archaic:

Infinitive		*Present*		
klä	**(kläda)**	**klär**	**(kläder)**	dress
bre	**(breda)**	**brer**	**(breder)**	spread
spä	**(späda)**	**spär**	**(späder)**	dilute
trä	**(träda)**	**trär**	**(träder)**	step

7.2.6 | Irregular verbs of the third conjugation

Irregular forms are marked *. Forms preceded by + exist only in compounds, e.g **nedgångna skor**, down-at-heel shoes.

Infinitive	Present	Past	Supine	Past participle	
be	**ber**	**bad***	**bett**	**+bedd**	ask
dö	**dör**	**dog***	**dött**	**–**	die
få	**får**	**fick***	**fått**	**–**	get
ge	**ger**	**gav***	**gett/givit**	**given**	give
gå	**går**	**gick***	**gått**	**+gången**	walk, go
le	**ler**	**log***	**lett**	**–**	smile
se	**ser**	**såg***	**sett**	**sedd**	see
stå	**står**	**stod***	**stått**	**stådd**	stand

Note: Two verbs of this group possess longer forms which are now formal or archaic:

Infinitive		*Present*	
ge	**(giva)**	**ger**	**(giver)**
be	**(bedja)**	**ber**	**(beder)**

Infinitive	Present	Past	Supine	Past participle	
-a	+er	Vowel change	Vowel change +it	+en	
dricka	**dricker**	**drack**	**druckit**	**drucken**	drink

This conjugation includes only strong verbs, i.e. those whose past tense is formed not by adding an ending but by changing the stem vowel. This vowel change often applies also to the supine:

flyga   flyger   flög   flugit   flugen   fly

Strong verbs are best learned individually, but many follow the same vowel change sequence or gradation series. The vowel is often the same in the infinitive/present and supine/past participle, and forms are largely predictable.

Notes:

1 Several strong verbs in this group possess longer forms which are now formal or archaic:

Infinitive		*Present*		
dra	**(draga)**	**drar**	**(drager)**	pull
ta	**(taga)**	**tar**	**(tager)**	take
bli	**(bliva)**	**blir**	**(bliver)**	be, become

2 The past tense of strong verbs until the early 1900s possessed a separate plural form in written Swedish which often had a different stem vowel from the singular. These forms (given in brackets) are now archaic:

blev (blevo), bjöd (bjödo), fann (funno), bar (buro), bad (bådo), var (voro)

7.2.8 *Fourth conjugation: gradation series i – e – i*

Irregular forms are marked *.

Infinitive	Present	Past	Supine	Past participle	
bita	**biter**	**bet**	**bitit**	**biten**	bite
bli*	**blir***	**blev**	**blivit**	**bliven**	be, become
driva	**driver**	**drev**	**drivit**	**driven**	drive, drift
glida	**glider**	**gled**	**glidit**	–	glide
gnida	**gnider**	**gned**	**gnidit**	**gniden**	rub
kliva	**kliver**	**klev**	**klivit**	–	step, climb
knipa	**kniper**	**knep**	**knipit**	–	pinch
kvida	**kvider**	**kved/**	**kvidit**	–	whimper
		***kvidde**			
lida	**lider**	**led**	**lidit**	**liden**	suffer
niga	**niger**	**neg**	**nigit**	–	curtsy
pipa	**piper**	**pep**	**pipit**	–	chirp
rida	**rider**	**red**	**ridit**	**riden**	ride
riva	**river**	**rev**	**rivit**	**riven**	tear
skina	**skiner**	**sken**	**skinit**	–	shine
skrida	**skrider**	**skred**	**skridit**	**skriden**	glide
skrika	**skriker**	**skrek**	**skrikit**	–	shout
skriva	**skriver**	**skrev**	**skrivit**	**skriven**	write
slita	**sliter**	**slet**	**slitit**	**sliten**	wear out
smita	**smiter**	**smet**	**smitit**	–	run away
sprida	**sprider**	**spred**	**spritt***	**spridd***	spread
			/spridit		
stiga	**stiger**	**steg**	**stigit**	**stigen**	step, climb
strida	**strider**	**stred**	**stridit/**	**stridd*/**	fight
		stridde	**stritt***		
svida	**svider**	**sved**	**svidit**	–	smart
svika	**sviker**	**svek**	**svikit**	**sviken**	fail, desert
tiga	**tiger**	**teg**	**tigit**	–	be silent
vika	**viker**	**vek**	**vikit/vikt**	**vikt/viken**	fold, yield
vina	**viner**	**ven**	**vinit**	–	whine
vrida	**vrider**	**vred**	**vridit**	**vriden**	twist

7.2.9 | Fourth conjugation: gradation series y̱/(j)u̱ – ö̱ – u̱

Irregular forms are marked *. Forms preceded by + exist only in compounds,
e.g. **en djupfryst kyckling,** a deep-frozen chicken.

Infinitive	Present	Past	Supine	Past participle	
bjuda	**bjuder**	**bjöd**	**bjudit**	**bjuden**	invite
bryta	**bryter**	**bröt**	**brutit**	**bruten**	break
drypa	**dryper**	**dröp**	**drupit/ drypt***	–	drip
duga	**duger**	**dög**	**dugt***	–	be suitable
dyka	**dyker**	**dök**	**dykt***	–	dive
flyga	**flyger**	**flög**	**flugit**	**flugen**	fly
flyta	**flyter**	**flöt**	**flutit**	**fluten**	float
frysa	**fryser**	**frös**	**frusit**	**frusen**	freeze (itr.), be cold
cf. 7.2.3	*fryser*	*fryste*	*fryst*	*+fryst*	*freeze (tr.)*
gjuta	**gjuter**	**göt***	**gjutit**	**gjuten**	cast (metal)
hugga	**hugger**	**högg**	**huggit**	**huggen**	chop
klyva	**klyver**	**klöv**	**kluvit**	**kluven**	cleave, split
knyta	**knyter**	**knöt**	**knutit**	**knuten**	tie, knot
krypa	**kryper**	**kröp**	**krupit**	**krupen**	creep
ljuda	**ljuder**	**ljöd**	**ljudit**	–	sound
ljuga	**ljuger**	**ljög**	**ljugit**	**ljugen**	tell a lie
njuta	**njuter**	**njöt**	**njutit**	**njuten**	enjoy
nypa	**nyper**	**nöp/ (nypte)***	**nupit/ (nypt)***	**nupen**	pinch
nysa	**nyser**	**nös**	**nyst***	–	sneeze
rysa	**ryser**	**rös**	**ryst***	–	shudder
ryta	**ryter**	**röt**	**rutit**	–	roar
sjuda	**sjuder**	**sjöd**	**sjudit**	**sjuden**	simmer
sjunga	**sjunger**	**sjöng**	**sjungit**	**sjungen**	sing

sjunka	sjunker	sjönk	sjunkit	sjunken	sink (itr.)
skjuta	skjuter	sköt*	skjutit	skjuten	shoot
skryta	skryter	skröt	skrutit	–	boast
sluta	sluter	slöt	slutit	sluten	close
cf.	*slutar*	*slutade*	*slutat*	*+slutad*	*end*
smyga	smyger	smög	smugit	smugen	slink
snyta	snyter	snöt	snutit	snuten	blow one's nose
stryka	stryker	strök	strukit	struken	stroke
strypa	stryper	ströp/ strypte	strypt	strypt	throttle
suga	suger	sög	sugit	sugen	suck
supa	super	söp	supit	supen	drink
tjuta	tjuter	tjöt	tjutit	–	howl
tryta	tryter	tröt	trutit	–	run short

7.2.10 *Fourth conjugation: gradation series i – a – u*

Forms preceded by + exist only in compounds, e.g. **en nedsutten hatt**, a sat-upon hat.

Infinitive	Present	Past	Supine	Past participle	
binda	binder	band	bundit	bunden	bind, tie
brinna	brinner	brann	brunnit	brunnen	burn (itr.)
brista	brister	brast	brustit	brusten	burst
dricka	dricker	drack	druckit	drucken	drink
finna	finner	fann	funnit	funnen	find
finnas	finns	fanns	funnits	–	be (located)
försvinna	försvinner	försvann	försvunnit	försvunnen	disappear
förnimma	förnimmer	förnam	förnummit	förnummen	perceive
hinna	hinner	hann	hunnit	–	have time
rinna	rinner	rann	runnit	runnen	run, flow

sitta	sitter	satt	suttit	+sutten	sit
slinka	slinker	slank	slunkit	–	slink
slinta	slinter	slant	(sluntit)	–	slip
slippa	slipper	slapp	sluppit	+sluppen	avoid
spinna	spinner	spann	spunnit	spunnen	spin, purr
spricka	spricker	sprack	spruckit	sprucken	crack, burst
springa	springer	sprang	sprungit	sprungen	run
sticka	sticker	stack	stuckit	stucken	sting
cf. 7.2.1	stickar	stickade	stickat	stickad	knit
stinka	stinker	stank	–	–	stink
vinna	vinner	vann	vunnit	vunnen	win

7.2.11 **Fourth conjugation: gradation series a̱ – o̱ – a̱**

Irregular forms are marked *.

Infinitive	Present	Past	Supine	Past participle	
dra*	drar*	drog	dragit	dragen	pull
fara	far*	for	farit	faren	travel
gala	gal*	gol	galit/galt	–	crow
ta*	tar*	tog	tagit	tagen	take

7.2.12 **Fourth conjugation: gradation series ä̱ – a̱ – u̱**

Irregular forms are marked *.

Infinitive	Present	Past	Supine	Past participle	
bära	bär*	bar	burit	buren	carry
skära	skär*	skar	skurit	skuren	cut
stjäla*	stjäl*	stal	stulit	stulen	steal
svälta	svälter	svalt	svultit	svulten	starve (itr.)
cf. 7.2.3		svälte	svält	svält	starve (tr.)

7.2.13 *Fourth conjugation: minor gradation series (mixed)*

Forms preceded by + exist only in compounds, e.g **en uppäten paj**, a pie that is eaten up.

Infinitive	Present	Past	Supine	Past participle	
falla	**faller**	**föll**	**fallit**	**fallen**	fall
gråta	**gråter**	**grät**	**gråtit**	**+gråten**	weep
hålla	**håller**	**höll**	**hållit**	**hållen**	hold
komma	**kommer**	**kom**	**kommit**	**kommen**	come
ligga	**ligger**	**låg**	**legat***	**+legad***	lie
låta	**låter**	**lät**	**låtit**	**+låten**	allow
slå	**slår**	**slog**	**slagit**	**slagen**	hit
slåss	**slåss**	**slogs**	**slagits**	–	fight
sova	**sover**	**sov**	**sovit**	–	sleep
svära	**svär**	**svor**	**svurit**	**svuren**	swear
vara	**är***	**var**	**varit**	–	be
äta	**äter**	**åt**	**ätit**	**+äten**	eat

7.3 Participles and supine

7.3.1 *Supine and past participle forms*

Conj.	Supine	Past participle Non-neuter	Neuter	Plural/Definite	
I	**älskat**	**älskad**	**älskat**	**älskade**	loved
IIa	**böjt**	**böjd**	**böjt**	**böjda**	bent
IIb	**köpt**	**köpt**	**köpt**	**köpta**	bought
III	**sytt**	**sydd**	**sytt**	**sydda**	sewn
IV	**bitit**	**biten**	**bitet**	**bitna**	bitten
	bjudit	**bjuden**	**bjudet**	**bjudna**	invited

Notes:

1 The supine is the same as the neuter form of the past participle in conjugations I, II, III.

2 In conjugation IV the supine ends in **-it** and the neuter past participle in **-et**.

3 Even in the non-neuter form IIb verbs have a past participle in **-t**.

7.3.2 | Use of the supine and past participle

1 The supine is used with **har/hade** to form the perfect and pluperfect tenses respectively. No other verbs are used before the supine. It does *not* inflect.

Olle har tvättat bilen.   Olle has washed the car.

Han hade tvättat den innan det började regna.
He had washed it before it began to rain.

2 The past participle is used as an adjective and inflects as follows (see also 4.2 ff, 7.3.1):

	Indefinite attributive	Definite attributive
Conj. I	**en nytvättad bil** a newly washed car	**den nytvättade bilen** the newly washed car
	bilen är nytvättad the car is newly washed	
	ett nymålat hus a newly painted house	**det nymålade huset** the newly painted house
	huset är nymålat the house is newly painted	
Conj. IIb	**en nyköpt lampa** a newly bought lamp	**den nyköpta lampan** the newly bought lamp
	lampan är nyköpt the lamp is newly bought	
	ett nyköpt bord a newly bought table	**det nyköpta bordet** the newly bought table
	bordet är nyköpt the table is newly bought	
Conj. IV	**en omskriven bok** a rewritten book	**den omskrivna boken** the rewritten book
	boken är omskriven the book is rewritten	
	ett omskrivet brev a rewritten letter	**det omskrivna brevet** the rewritten letter
	brevet är omskrivet the letter is rewritten	

Note: The past participle is also used with forms of **vara** or **bli** to construct one type of passive. See 7.5.17.

7.3.3 | Present participle

Form

Verbs with *stem* ending in:	*Present participle* consists of:
a *consonant* or -a (Conj. I, II, IV):	stem + (a)nde:
	ropande, ringande, skrivande
a *long vowel*	stem + ende:
(Conj. III and many irregular verbs):	**troende, stående**

Use

1 Present participles are only rarely used in Swedish like the English '-ing' forms, notably after the verbs **komma, gå, bli** and verbs of motion:

De kom springande. They came running.

Han blev sittande/liggande. He remained sitting/lying.

Sjungande Internationalen marscherade studenterna genom gatorna.
Singing the Internationale the students marched through the streets.

2 Normally the present participle is used in one of the following ways:

(a) An adjective: **en heltäckande matta, en genomgripande förändring**
(b) A noun: **ett erbjudande, ett påstående, en studerande**
(c) An adverb: **Han var påfallande lat. Vädret var övervägande mulet.**
(d) A preposition: **Angående/Beträffande/Rörande det här fallet . . .**

7.4 Translating verbs

7.4.1 | Some problems in translating English verbs

These notes isolate only very common problems. They are not dictionary definitions.

Arrive/leave

1 arrive [of people] **anlända, komma**

The students arrive today. **Studenterna kommer idag.**

2 arrive [of trains, boats, planes, etc.] **ankomma**

The plane gets in at
eight (o'clock).

**Flygplanet ankommer
klockan åtta.**

3 leave [intransitive] **avgå, resa, åka, gå**

They left early.

De gick tidigt.

4 leave [transitive] **lämna**

They left their car in the
car park.

**De lämnade bilen i
parkeringen.**

Ask

1 enquire **fråga**

We asked him what he
was called.

**Vi frågade honom
vad han hette.**

2 ask [someone to do something] **be**

We asked him to come.

Vi bad honom komma.

3 ask [questions] **ställa**

The police asked us a lot
of questions.

Polisen ställde en massa frågor.

Change

1 alter **ändra, förändra**

The law has changed
recently.

Lagen ändrades nyligen.

2 change one's mind **ändra sig**

He changed his mind
several times.

Han ändrade sig flera gånger.

3 exchange [something for something else: e.g. clothes] **byta**

He changed trains at
Hallsberg.

Han bytte tåg i Hallsberg.

4 change gear, change money **växla**

The driver changed down.   **Föraren växlade ner.**

Drive

1 drive a vehicle [i.e. sit behind the wheel] **köra**

Olle drives a bus.   **Olle kör buss.**

2 travel [i.e. be driven]   **åka**

We drove to Norway   **Vi åkte till Norge i sommar.**
this summer.

3 provide the power for something **driva**

What is it that drives him on?   **Vad är det som driver honom?**

Feel

1 feel [transitive] **känna**

Suddenly he felt the pain.   **Plötsligt kände han smärtan.**

2 feel [intransitive] **känna sig**

He felt tired.   **Han kände sig trött.**

3 feel [i.e. 'is experienced as': deponent] **kännas**

It feels cold.   **Det känns kallt.**

Go

1 go by vehicle **åka, resa, fara**

I am going to America.   **Jag reser till Amerika.**

2 go [generally; esp. walk, leave] **gå**

I really must go.   **Jag måste verkligen gå.**

Grow

1 grow [intransitive] **växa**

Rice grows in China.   **Ris växer i Kina.**

2 grow [transitive] **odla**

People grow rice in China.   **Folk odlar ris i Kina.**

3 increase in size **öka**

The number is growing all the time.   **Antalet ökar ständigt.**

Know

1 know [facts] **veta**

Do you know what he is called?   **Vet du vad han heter?**

2 know [people] **känna**

Do you know him?   **Känner du honom?**

3 **know** [languages, specialisms] **kunna**

Do you know French?   **Kan du franska?**

Live

1 dwell, reside **bo**

He lives in Stockholm.   **Han bor i Stockholm.**

2 be alive **leva**

Linné lived in the 18th century.   **Linné levde på 1700-talet.**

Put

1 place horizontally **lägga**

Put the book on the table!   **Lägg boken på bordet!**

2 place upright **ställa**

Put the bottle on the table!   **Ställ flaskan på bordet!**

3 fix **sätta**

Put the curtains up!   **Sätt upp gardinerna!**

4 insert into **stoppa**

Don't put your hands in   **Stoppa inte händerna i**
your pockets!   **fickorna!**

See

1 see **se**

Can you see the lighthouse   **Kan du se fyrtornet**
from here?   **härifrån?**

2 meet **träffa**

There's a Mr Smith to   **En herr Smith vill träffa dig.**
see you.

Stop

1 movement **stanna**

She stopped the car.   **Hon stannade bilen.**

2 cease doing **sluta**

He stopped talking.   **Han slutade tala.**

Think

1 hold an opinion **tycka**

I think it's a boring film.   **Jag tycker att det är en tråkig**
                                        film.

2 ponder **tänka**

She sat thinking about it.   **Hon satt och tänkte på det.**

3 intend **tänka**

He is thinking of buying a car.   **Jag tänker köpa en bil.**

4 believe **tro**

I think it might rain.　　　　**Jag tror att det kommer att regna.**

Want

1 want (to do) **vilja**

I want to go home　　　　**Jag vill gå hem.**

2 want (to have) **vilja ha**

I want a new car.　　　　**Jag vill ha en ny bil.**

| 7.4.2 | *Translating the English verb 'to be'* |

No fewer than five Swedish verbs other than **vara** are used to translate different senses of the English verb 'to be'.

In order to indicate location three verbs are often used in preference to **vara**, namely **ligga** (main meaning = lie), **sitta** (main meaning = sit) and **stå** (main meaning = stand).

1 **ligga**

(a) Used of towns, buildings and places:

Sverige ligger i Skandinavien.	Sweden is in Scandinavia.
Staden ligger vid en liten sjö.	The town is/lies by a little lake.
I centrum ligger många banker.	In the centre there are many banks.

(b) Used of objects which lie horizontally:

Var ska tidningen ligga?
Where should the newspaper be/go?

Kläderna låg utströdda på golvet.
The clothes lay strewn across the floor.

(c) Notice also:

Hans son låg vid universitetet.	His son was at university.
Jag låg och läste. (= Jag läste)	I was (lay) reading.

119

2 sitta

(a) Used of objects that are fixed in position:

Tavlorna sitter snett.	The pictures are crooked.
Sitter nyckeln i låset?	Is the key in the lock?
Muttern sitter fast.	The nut is stuck.
Dina glasögon sitter på näsan.	Your glasses are on your nose.

(b) Notice also:

Olle sitter i fängelse/i sammanträde/i en kommitté.
Olle is in prison/at a meeting/on a committee.

Jag satt och drack te.	I was/sat drinking tea.

3 stå

(a) Used of objects that stand vertically:

Var ska skåpet stå?	Where should the cupboard stand?
Bordet står i hörnet.	The table is/stands in the corner.
Står inte boken på hyllan?	Isn't the book on the shelf?

(b) = be (written):

Detta står på sidan 10 i boken.	That is on page 10 of the book.

4 To indicate transition (change of state) or existence, two verbs are used in preference to **vara**, namely **bli** (indicating transition) and **finnas** (indicating existence):

(a) **bli** (transition)

Vad tänker du bli när du har tagit din examen?
What do you intend to be when you have graduated?

Han blir sju år idag.	He will be seven today.

Han blev förvånad över att höra nyheten.
He was surprised to hear the news.

Bli inte arg!	Don't get angry!
Vad blev resultatet?	What was the result?

(b) **finnas** (existence)

Det finns många sjöar i Sverige.
There are a lot of lakes in Sweden.

I Uppsala finns det en domkyrka.
In Uppsala there is a cathedral.

7.5 The use of the infinitive and different verbal constructions

7.5.1 Infinitive – verbal use

1 In two-verb constructions after the modal auxiliaries **kan, ska, vill, måste,** etc. (7.5.10–7.5.11):

Han kan komma ikväll.	He can come tonight.
Måste du göra det?	Do you have to do that?
Får jag följa med?	May I come along?
Ska du åka bort över jul?	Are you going away over Christmas?
Vill du åka bort?	Do you want to go away?

2 In two-verb constructions after modal equivalents:

De brukar åka bort.	They usually go away.
Jag hoppas kunna åka.	I hope to be able to go away.
Hon tänker inte gifta sig.	She doesn't intend to get married.
Det verkar vara sant.	It appears to be true.

Modal equivalents include:

behöva	need	**råka**	happen to
bruka	usually do	**slippa**	avoid
börja	begin	**sluta**	stop
fortsätta	continue	**tyckas**	seem to
försöka	try to	**tänka**	intend to
hoppas	hope to	**verka**	appear to

lova	promise (to)	**våga**	dare to
lyckas	succeed in	**vägra**	refuse to
låtsas	pretend to	**ämna**	intend to
orka	manage to	**önska**	wish to

Notes:

1 After the following verbs **att** is optional: **börjar** (att), begin; **försöker** (att), try; **slutar** (att), stop

2 In spoken Swedish and informal language there is a tendency to omit **att** after **kommer** (cf. 7.5.9):

Han kommer inte vinna i år.   He will not win this year.

3 In object + infinitive constructions, often with the verbs **se** (see), **höra** (hear), **låta** (allow, let), **tillåta** (permit), **anse** (consider):

Vi såg honom göra det.   We saw him do it.

Jag hörde henne sjunga.   I heard her sing.

Han lät kaffet kallna.   He allowed the coffee to cool.

4 In reflexive object + infinitive constructions, often with the verbs **säga sig** (say), **påstå sig** (claim), **förklara sig** (declare), **tro sig** (consider), **anse sig** (consider):

Hon säger sig vara lycklig.   She says that she is happy.

7.5.2 *Infinitive – nominal use*

Infinitive phrases (**att** + infinitive) often function as if they were noun phrases:

1 As the subject:

Att bada i havet är skönt.
Swimming in the sea is wonderful.

Det är skönt att bada i havet.
It is wonderful to swim in the sea. (see 12.7.7)

Note that the predicative adjective is inflected as if it referred to a neuter singular noun and that **det** is often found as a formal anticipatory subject.

2 As the object:

Hon älskar att köra bil. She loves driving/to drive.

3 After a preposition or a stressed verb particle:

Han gick utan att säga någonting.
He left without saying anything.

Jag tycker om att läsa rysare.
I like reading thrillers.

Du måste tänka på att byta jobb.
You must think of changing jobs.

Note that in expressions indicating an intention **för att** is used:

Han kom hit för att vila sig. He came here (in order) to rest.

4 When qualifying a noun or pronoun:

Konsten att skriva. The art of writing.

Jag har ingenting att säga. I have nothing to say.

7.5.3 | Use of the infinitive in English and Swedish

1 English infinitive = Swedish infinitive. The use of the infinitive in the two languages is often identical, notably in two-verb constructions (see 7.5.1, 7.5.4), adjectival constructions and in certain object and infinitive constructions.

You really must hurry. **Ni måste verkligen skynda er.**

It's not easy to do that. **Det är inte lätt att göra det.**

They saw me come back. **De såg mig komma tillbaka.**

2 However, Swedish often has a full clause when English has object + infinitive after verbs like 'want' or 'wish' (NB: **att** is a conjunction here), after 'wait/long for', 'count/rely on', and after an interrogative:

What do you want me to do? **Vad vill du att jag skall göra?**

They waited for the rain to stop.
De väntade på att regnet skulle upphöra.

They don't know what to do. **De vet inte vad de ska göra.**

123

7.5.4 Translating '-ing' forms

1 For the English continuous (or progressive) tense see 7.5.5 (3).

2 English infinitive or gerund ('-ing' form) = Swedish infinitive (see also 7.5.1 f):

He began to write/writing.	**Han började skriva.**
It's no use trying.	**Det är inte värt att försöka.**
He left without saying goodbye.	**Han gick utan att säga adjö.**

3 English gerund ('-ing' form) = Swedish full clause:

He admits having stolen the car.
Han medger att han har stulit bilen.

We thanked him for coming.
Vi tackade honom för att han kom.

7.5.5 Present tense

1 The present tense is used much as in English. It has five main uses:

(a) Present action:

Jag sitter hemma nu och läser tidningen.
I'm sitting at home reading the paper.

(b) Universal action:

Jorden går runt solen.	The Earth goes round the Sun.

(c) Repeated action:

Lektionerna börjar klockan 9.	Lessons start at 9 o'clock.

(d) Future action:

Om en vecka reser jag bort. (See also 7.5.9.)
In a week's time I'm going away.

(e) Historic present (to create an illusion of present):

27 november bryter Strindberg upp från Klam och reser över Berlin och Danmark hem.
On 27 November Strindberg leaves Klam and travels home via Berlin and Denmark.

2 Notice the following minor difference of usage:

Present in Swedish = past in English when an action is completed in the past but a tangible result remains:

När är du född?   When were you born?

Jag är född 1951.   I was born in 1951.
(cf. **När** *var* **Napoleon född?** – when a person is dead)

Slottet är byggt på 1300-talet.
The castle was built in the 14th century.

3 The English continuous (or progressive) tense with forms in '-ing' corresponds in Swedish to:

(a) Simple present tense

I am sitting in my study.   **Jag sitter på arbetsrummet.**

I am sitting reading.   **Jag sitter och läser.**

(b) **Håller på att** + infinitive, which is used to stress the continuity of an action:

He is (busy) painting the bathroom.
Han håller på att måla badrummet.

I'm (in the process of) learning Greek.
Jag håller på att lära mig grekiska.

7.5.6	*Past tense*

Sometimes known as the imperfect or preterite tense, the past tense in Swedish is used much as in English, namely to express an action completed at a point of time in the past.

1 The past tense is often used in conjunction with a time marker, often an adverb:

I fjol/Då reste vi till Grekland.
Last year/Then we went to Greece.

2 The past tense may express a repeated action:

Som liten skrek han ofta.
As a small child he yelled a lot.

125

3 The past tense may inject a note of politeness or caution into a demand or intention, especially with the modal auxiliary (see 7.5.11):

Jag skulle vilja ha en sådan, tack.	I would like one of those, please.
(Cf. **Jag vill ha . . .**	I want . . .)
Kunde du möjligen hjälpa mig?	Could you possibly help me?
(Cf. **Kan du . . .**	Can you . . .)

4 The past tense may possess a modal sense (see 7.5.11):

Om jag hade tid skulle jag skriva en bok.
If I had time I would write a book.

5 Swedish past tense = English present tense in exclamations and on first impressions:

Det var snällt av dig att komma.	It is kind of you to come.
Detta var verkligen gott!	This is really good!

7.5.7 | Perfect tense

The perfect tense is formed by using **har** with the supine (see 7.3.2). The verb **har** is often omitted in the subordinate clause in written Swedish:

Då jag inte (har) fått svar på mitt brev, skriver jag igen.
As I have not received a reply to my letter, I am writing again.

The perfect tense in Swedish is, as in English, used to indicate a link between past and present, the relevance of a completed action in the past to a present situation:

Vi har alltid rest till Spanien förr, men nu föredrar vi Grekland.
We have always gone to Spain before, but now we prefer Greece.

The tense indicates an indeterminate length of time or point in time but the point of reference is usually the present.

1 Time markers are used to indicate present time:

Nu har jag avslutat boken.
Now I have finished the book.

2 As in English the perfect may indicate that an action has taken place and is still taking place:

De har varit gifta i många år.
They have been married for many years.

3 Unlike English the perfect may express future:

Om en månad har vi glömt/kommer vi att ha glömt allting.
In a month we will have forgotten everything.

4 Perfect in Swedish = past in English, when the present result is emphasized rather than the action in the past:

Vem har skrivit Röda rummet?	Who wrote 'The Red Room'?
Var har du lärt dig svenska?	Where did you learn Swedish?
Det har jag aldrig tänkt på.	I never thought of that.

7.5.8	*Pluperfect tense*

The pluperfect tense is formed by using **hade** with the supine (see 7.3.2). The verb **hade** is often omitted in the subordinate clause in written Swedish:

Om jag inte (hade) hittat boken vet jag inte vad jag hade gjort.
If I hadn't found the book I don't know what I would have done.

The pluperfect tense is used much as in English. It expresses an action that took place before an action expressed by the past tense:

Innan han kom hit hade han köpt blommor.
Before he came here he had bought some flowers.

Other uses:

1 The pluperfect tense may express the result of a completed action:

Då hade vi redan gett upp allt hopp.
By then we had already given up all hope.

2 The pluperfect may indicate that an action had taken place and at some point in the past was still taking place:

De hade varit gifta i många år när de skildes.
They had been married for many years when they got divorced.

3 The pluperfect may have a modal sense (see 7.5.11) indicating an unreal situation:

> **Om det bara inte varit så halt på vägen hade jag klarat mig.**
> If only it hadn't been so icy on the road I would have been all right.

7.5.9 | *Future tense*

There are three ways of expressing the future in Swedish:

1 Present tense + time marker is the most common construction. **Blir** is often used instead of **är** in this instance:

Jag åker snart.	I'll be going soon.
I år reser vi utomlands.	This year we are going abroad.
Det gör jag imorgon.	I'll do that tomorrow.
Det blir ljust om en timme.	It will be light in an hour.

2 **Kommer att** + infinitive is objective and often (but not always) found with an impersonal subject:

> **Det kommer att regna ikväll.**
> It is going to rain tonight.

> **Ni kommer att bli förvånade.**
> You will be surprised.

Increasingly **att** is omitted:

> **Denna fråga kommer bli viktigare i framtiden.**
> This issue will become more important in the future.

3 **Ska** + infinitive often indicates intention and is often found with a personal subject:

Jag ska titta på TV ikväll.	I am going to watch TV tonight.
Ska du resa imorgon?	Are you leaving tomorrow?

Notice, however, that **ska** + infinitive may on occasion be objective when used with an impersonal subject:

Det ska bli auktion.	There is going to be an auction.
(= Det blir/kommer att bli auktion.)	

7.5.10 Mood and modal verbs

The attitude of the speaker to the activity contained in the verb is expressed by one of the following:

Modal verb + main verb (infinitive, 7.5.1):

Vi måste springa.   We must run.

Subjunctive (7.5.12):

Det vore roligt att träffa honom. It would be nice to meet him.

Imperative (7.5.13):

Gå ut härifrån!   Get out of here!

Modal verbs have irregular forms:

Infinitive	Present	Past	Supine	
kunna	**kan**	**kunde**	**kunnat**	be able
skola	**ska(ll)**	**skulle**	**skolat**	shall, will
vilja	**vill**	**ville**	**velat**	will, want to
–	**måste**	**måste**	**måst**	must, have to
böra	**bör**	**borde**	**bort**	should, ought to
–	–	**torde**	–	is probably
–	**må**	–	–	may, must
–	**måtte**	–	–	may, must
–	**lär**	–	–	is said to
låta	**låter**	**lät**	**låtit**	let
få	**får**	**fick**	**fått**	may, be allowed to, must, have to

7.5.11 Use of modal verbs

1 ska (or **skall**) (past tense **skulle**)

(a) Future: see 7.5.9.

(b) Conditional:

Om jag hade tid, skulle jag resa. If I had time, I would go away.
Jag skulle knappast tro det.   I would scarcely believe it.

(c) Polite use (use past tense):

Jag skulle vilja be dig om en tjänst.   I would like to ask a favour.

NB: **Ska** often translates English 'will'. See 7.5.9.

2 vill (past tense **ville**)

(a) 'want to, will': *Never* simple future, cf. 7.5.9.

Jag vill åka utomlands.	I want to go abroad.
(Cf. **Ska de åka utomlands?**	Are they going abroad?)

But, note:

Will you give me a hand with this?   **Vill du hjälpa mig med detta?**

(b) 'would like', 'would have liked' when followed in Swedish by **ha**:

Vill du ha ett glas öl?   Would you like a glass of beer?
i.e. Will you have a glass of beer?

(c) Polite use (especially when past tense is chosen):

Jag ville helst inte stanna.   I would rather not stay.

3 måste

(a) Compulsion – 'must/have to' in positive expressions:

Jag måste tyvärr sluta nu.
I have to finish now, unfortunately.

(b) Concession – 'do not have/need to' in negative expressions:

Du måste ju inte äta så mycket!
You don't have/need to eat so much.

Cf. 'Must not' (prohibition) is expressed by **får inte**:

Du får inte äta så mycket!
You must not eat so much!

4 bör, borde

Suitability:

Du borde få lite frisk luft.
You ought to/should get some fresh air.

5 kan, kunde

(a) Possibility:

Vi kan följa med ikväll.   We can/are able to come along tonight.

(b) Ability:

Eva kan köra bil.   Eva can drive.

(c) Concession:

Det kan du ha rätt i.   You may be right about that.

7.5.12 Subjunctive

The subjunctive is rare in Swedish now. It is generally found only in the form **vore** (from **vara**) and in some fixed expressions:

Det vore roligt om du kunde följa med.
It would be nice if you could come.

Tack vare din hjälp . . .   Thanks to your help . . .

Leve konungen!   Long live the King!

Gud bevare oss!   God help us!

7.5.13 Imperative

1 Form: The imperative is the same as the stem. This means that it is the same as the infinitive for conjugations I and III and the infinitive minus -a for conjugations II and IV. Imperatives are often followed by an exclamation mark in Swedish.

	Imperative		cf. Infinitive
I	**Arbeta hårdare!**	Work harder!	**arbeta**
IIa	**Släng bort den!**	Throw it away!	**slänga**
IIb	**Hjälp mig!**	Help me!	**hjälpa**
II irr.	**Gör något!**	Do something!	**göra**
III	**Tro mig eller inte!**	Believe me or not!	**tro**
III irr.	**Gå hem!**	Go home!	**gå**
IV	**Skriv ett brev!**	Write a letter!	**skriva**
IV	**Var inte dum nu!**	Don't be stupid now!	**vara**

131

2 Use: The imperative expresses a command, wish or piece of advice. Occasionally the subject is inserted in spoken Swedish, especially to underline a contrast:

Kom hit du, så ska vi dricka kaffe.
You come here and we'll have coffee.

Sitt kvar du, så städar jag.
You sit there and I'll tidy up.

Notice the difference in the position of the subject, when inserted, between Swedish and English:

Sitt kvar du ...		You sit there ...	
FV	S	S	FV

3 Notice the following polite uses of the imperative:

Var snäll och ge mig ett äpple!	Please give me an apple.
Ge mig ett äpple är du snäll!	
Var så god och stig in!	Please come in!

7.5.14 Transitive, intransitive and reflexive verbs

1 *Transitive* verbs have a direct object (12.6.6):

John köpte huset.	John bought the house.

Intransitive verbs do not have a direct object:

John sov gott.	John slept well.

Ditransitive verbs have both an indirect and direct object (12.6.6):

John gav henne boken.	John gave her the book.

Reflexive verbs are intransitive, as the subject does not direct the action outwards (cf. transitive) but at itself:

Han tvättade sig. He washed (himself).
S ←——————

2 Whereas Swedish makes firm distinctions between transitive and intransitive verbs, many English verbs may be either:

They burn the paper.	**De bränner pappret.** (tr.)
The house burns down.	**Huset brinner ned.** (itr.)

Mary left the letter.   **Mary lämnade brevet.** (tr.)

Mary left early.   **Mary gick tidigt.** (itr.)

Other pairs of transitive/intransitive verbs in Swedish are:

Intransitive		Transitive	
sitta IV	sit	**sätta** IIrr	put
ligga IV	lie	**lägga** IIrr	lay
sjunka IV	sink	**sänka** IIb	sink
spräcka IIb	burst	**spricka** IV	burst
falla IV	fall	**fälla** IIa	fell
kallna I	grow cold, cool	**kyla** IIa	chill, cool
vaka I	stay awake	**väcka** IIb	awaken, arouse
vakna I	wake up		
ryka IIb	(give off) smoke	**röka** IIb	smoke
tröttna I	be tired, tire	**trötta** I	make tired, tire

3 A sizeable group of ditransitive verbs (with two objects) includes: **berätta**, tell; **visa**, show; **bjuda**, offer; **ge**, give; **lova**, promise, **låna**, lend; **räcka**, hand, **skicka**, send, **skänka**, donate; **säga**, tell; **sända**, send

4 Many reflexive verbs in Swedish are not reflexive in English:

Vi ska tvätta/raka/kamma oss.

We shall wash/shave/comb our hair.

De gifte sig förra året.

They got married last year.

Per reste sig och sedan satte sig igen.

Per got up and then he sat down again.

Hon klädde sig i svart.

She dressed in black.

For reflexive pronouns see 5.1, 5.3.

5 Many reflexive verbs indicate movement:

lägga sig	lie down	**förkyla sig**	catch a cold
röra sig	move	**lära sig**	learn
bege sig	go	**känna sig**	feel
vända sig	turn round	**förirra sig**	get lost
infinna sig	present oneself	**skynda sig**	hurry up
närma sig	approach		

7.5.15 s-forms

	Infinitive	Present	Past	Supine	
I	**bakas**	**bakas**	**bakades**	**bakats**	be baked
IIa	**böjas**	**böjs**	**böjdes**	**böjts**	be bent
IIb	**köpas**	**köps**	**köptes**	**köpts**	be bought
IIb -stem in **-s**:					
	läsas	**läses**	**lästes**	**lästs**	be read
III	**sys**	**sys**	**syddes**	**sytts**	be sewn
IV	**bjudas**	**bjuds**	**bjöds**	**bjudits**	be invited

In most cases the -s is simply added to the end of the active form, but notice especially how to form the present tense:

> **bakar** + s → **bakas** (i.e. delete present tense ending first)
>
> **köper** + s → **köps**
>
> **säljer** + s → **säljs**

Formal written Swedish retains the -e however:

> **köper** + s → **köpes**

7.5.16 Uses of s-forms

1 Passive (see 7.5.17):

Huset målades.   The house was (being) painted.

2 Deponent: The deponent is active and intransitive, i.e. it has passive form but active meaning:

Jag hoppas att de lyckas.   I hope they succeed.

Vi trivs här.   We like it here.

Deponent verbs do not usually possess a form without -s. Deponents include:

minnas IIa	remember	**kräkas** IIb	vomit
finnas IV	be, exist	**umgås** IV	be friendly with
låtsas I	pretend	**trängas** IIa	push
synas IIb	appear	**töras** IIa	dare
tyckas IIb	seem	**envisas** I	persist
hoppas I	hope	**trivas** IIa	like it

3 Reciprocal: The reciprocal has a plural subject which both carries out an action and is the object of an action:

Vi träffas kl. 2. (= träffar varandra)
We will meet at 2 o'clock.

De kysstes bakom cykelstället.
They kissed behind the bicycle shed.

Other reciprocal verbs:

brottas I	wrestle	**kramas** I	hug (one another)
enas I	agree	**ses** IV	meet, rendezvous
följas åt IIa	accompany (one another)	**skiljas åt** IIa	part
hjälpas åt IIb	help (one another)	**slåss** IV	fight
höras IIa	be in touch (with one another)	**talas vid** I	talk over

135

7.5.17 Passive

Whereas active verbs often have a subject and an object, passive verbs have a subject and an agent:

Passive transformation:

Active	**Eva körde bilen.**	Eva drove the car.
	S ———→O	
Passive	**Bilen kördes av Eva.**	The car was driven by Eva.
	S ←———————AGENT	

Many passive verbs have no agent, however:

Bilen kördes vårdslöst.   The car was driven carelessly.

The reason is that the agent in many cases is unknown, unimportant or obvious from the context, and it is the action expressed by the verb or the object of that action (subject of the passive) which is the dominating idea:

Lunch serveras kl. 11.   Lunch is served at 11 o'clock.

Han dödades i en bilolycka.   He was killed in a car accident.

Mötet hålls i salen.   The meeting is being held in the hall.

Passives with an agent are more common in impersonal written Swedish:

Skiftnyckeln uppfanns av en svensk.
The adjustable spanner was invented by a Swede.

There are three ways of expressing the passive:

S-passive:	**Äpplena skalas.**
Forms of **bli** + past participle:	**Äpplena blir skalade.**
Forms of **vara** + past participle:	**Äpplena var skalade.**

Forms with **bli/vara** are sometimes called 'periphrastic forms'.

Use of passive forms

1 s-passive

This is by far the most common form, especially in written Swedish, and stresses the action of the verb, often indicating a repetition, command or instruction:

Frukost serveras kl. 9.
Breakfast is served at 9 o'clock.

Ordet uttalas med accent I.
The word is pronounced with accent I.

Felparkering straffas med böter.
Illegal parking is punishable by fine.

Öppnas här.
Open here. (E.g. on packages)

The s-passive construction often has no agent, and is often the equivalent of an active construction using **man, de, någon** or **folk:**

Nedrustning diskuteras. = **Man diskuterar nedrustning.**

Han anses vara frisk. = **Man anser honom vara frisk.**

2 bli-passive

This form stresses the action of the verb and often indicates an isolated occurrence. The **bli**-passive often has an agent.

Han blev påkörd av en bil.
He was run down by a car.

Vi blev avbrutna av servitrisen.
We were interrupted by the waitress.

Rekordet blev slaget av en svensk.
The record was beaten by a Swede.

Notice that **blir** (present tense) indicates future action (see 7.5.9):

Saken blir avgjord imorgon.
The matter will be decided tomorrow.

3 vara-passive

This form stresses a state, the result of an action, and the past participle is adjectival. It provides a static picture.

Himlen är täckt av moln. The sky is covered in cloud.

Han är bortrest för tillfället. He is away at present.

Huset är sålt. The house is/has been sold.

Väskan är stulen. The bag is/has been stolen.

4 Tense equivalents

Notice the following different ways of expressing the same idea:

vara-passive	*bli*-passive/*s*-passive
Present:	= Perfect:
Middagen är förstörd.	= **Middagen har blivit förstörd/ har förstörts.**
Vi är bjudna på fest.	= **Vi har blivit bjudna/ har bjudits på fest.**
Past:	= Pluperfect:
Middagen var förstörd.	= **Middagen hade blivit förstörd/ hade förstörts.**

5 Verbs often found in the passive (given below in the tenses in which they frequently occur):

anses, is considered; **betraktas**, is regarded; **byggdes**, was built; **diskuterades (diskuterats)**, was (has been) discussed; **dömdes**, was sentenced; **åtalas (åtalats)**, is (has been) charged; **gripits**, has been arrested; **nämnas (nämnts)**, is (has been) named; **publiceras**, is punished; **rapporteras**, is reported; **uppges**, is stated; **sändes**, was sent; **stängdes**, was closed; **såldes**, was sold; **utsågs**, was appointed

6 Differences in use between Swedish and English:

(a) English passive = Swedish active:

  (i) 'There' + passive = Swedish active form:

There was nothing to be done. **Det var inget att göra.**

  (ii) 'Be said to/reputed to' = Swedish **lär/ska**:

The food there is said to be good. **Maten där lär vara god.**

  (iii) English passive = Swedish **man** + active:

It is more difficult than is generally supposed.
Det är svårare än man i allmänhet tror.

(b) Swedish passive = English active:

    (i) **Det** + passive ('impersonal passive') = 'There is/was' + gerund (i.e. 'ing-' form):

Det dansades hela natten.   There was dancing all night.

    (ii) Some Swedish agentless passives = English intransitive verbs:

Dörren öppnades.   The door opened.

7.5.18 Compound verbs

Compound verbs are those prefixed by a particle.

In inseparable compounds the particle always remains attached:

Han betalar räkningen.   He pays the bill.

In separable compounds the particle may become separated from the verb:

Värmen är avstängd.   The heating is turned off.

Han stängde av värmen.   He turned off the heating.

1 *Inseparable* compounds include:

(a) Most verbs compounded with nouns, adjectives, other verbs and **själv-**:

hungerstrejka, godkänna, brännmärka, självdö

(b) Verbs with the following prefixes:

Unstressed prefixes:	**betala, *förklara***
Stressed prefixes:	***bistå*, erhålla, *föredra*, *missunna*, *närvara*, oroa, *samtycka*, *umgås*, *undkomma*, *vantrivas*, *välsigna***

2 *Separable* compounds include:

Many phrasal verbs with separable prefixes or particles. The particles, not the verbs, are always stressed:

resa *bort*, frysa *fast*, gå *förbi*, ta *ifrån*, känna *igen*, gå *igenom*, slå *ihjäl*, räkna *in*, följa *med*, lägga *ned*, tycka *om*, falla *omkull*, slå *sönder*, stryka *under*, slå *upp*, dricka *ur*, dö *ut*, gå *vilse*

These verbs are always compounded in the participial forms:

Han blev *ihjälslagen*.	He was killed.
Han är *bortrest*.	He has gone away.
ett *igen*kännande leende	a smile of recognition
en *omtyckt* rektor	a popular headteacher
en *ned*lagd fabrik	a closed factory

The same word may often be both a stressed particle and an unstressed preposition:

Han satte *på* tvn.	He put the TV on.
Han satte *tvn* på bordet.	He put the TV on the table.

3 Stylistic differences between separable and inseparable compound verbs:

Often the separated form is used in everyday language while the integral form is reserved for more formal written style.

Han lade ner böckerna på bordet.
He laid the books on the table.

Kungen nedlade en krans på graven.
The king laid a wreath on the grave.

Vi steg ner i gruvan.
We went down into the mine.

Kristus har nedstigit till dödsriket.
Christ has descended into Hell.

Hon lade fram hans pyjamas.
She laid out his pyjamas.

Hon framlade ett bra förslag.
She put forward a good proposal.

4 Semantic differences between separable and inseparable compound verbs:

Often the separated forms are concrete and the integral forms abstract in meaning. In some cases the semantic difference is so great as to warrant regarding the forms as two distinct verbs.

Jag bryter av grenen.   I break off the branch.

Jag avbryter samtalet. I interrupt the conversation.

Han strök under ordet. He underlined the word.

Han underströk ordets betydelse.
He emphasized the meaning of the word.

Lampan lyste upp rummet.
The lamp lit up the room.

De upplyste mig om mitt misstag.
They enlightened me as to my mistake.

5 Word order: (see also 12.6.7, 12.9.1 (8))

Notice that only a clausal adverbial (12.6.4, 12.6.7, 12.6.9) and/or a subject in inverted clauses may come between the verb and its separated particle, unlike English:

Kasta inte ut den! Don't throw it out!

Kastade de inte ut den? Didn't they throw it out?

Chapter 8

Adverbs

8.1 Forms of adverbs

1 Many adverbs derive from adjectives by adding the ending **-t**:

Hon var mycket vacker (*adj.*).   She was very beautiful.

Hon sjöng mycket vackert (*adv.*).   She sang very beautifully.

The adverb in **-t** is identical to the neuter form of the adjective in **-t**:

Huset var mycket vackert (*adj.*).   The house was very beautiful.

Huset var vackert (*adv.*)   The house was beautifully
målat.   painted.

2 Some adjectives ending in **-lig** form adverbs by adding **-en** or **-tvis**:

Han kommer möjligen   He is probably coming
imorgon.   tomorrow.

Naturligtvis talar han svenska.   Naturally he speaks Swedish.

Notice that forms in **-en, -tvis** are often clausal adverbials (see 12.6.4), whilst forms in **-t** are other adverbials of manner (see 12.6.5):

Han är lyckligt gift.   He is happily married.

Han är lyckligtvis gift.   Happily/Fortunately he is married.

3 Other adverbs which are derivatives include those ending in:

-städes/-stans (location):	**annorstädes, någonstans**	elsewhere, somewhere
-ledes/-lunda (manner):	**således, annorlunda**	thus, differently
-sin (time):	**någonsin**	ever
-vart (direction):	**någonvart**	somewhere

4 Many common adverbs are not derivatives, and these include:

(a) Adverbs of time: **aldrig** (never), **alltid** (always), **då** (then), **förr** (before), **genast** (immediately), **ibland** (sometimes), **igen** (again), **nu** (now), **ofta** (often), **strax** (shortly)

(b) Adverbs of place: **här/hit** (here), **där/dit** (there), **var/vart** (where), **hem** (home), **bort** (away), **fram** (forward), **in** (in), **ner** (down) (for usage see 8.3.)

(c) Adverbs of manner: **bra** (well), **fort** (quickly), **ganska** (rather), **precis** (exactly)

(d) Modal adverbs: **ju, nog, väl** (for meanings and usage see 8.4(7)), **inte** (not)

(e) Conjunctional adverbs: **alltså** (therefore), **också** (also), **så** (so)

5 Negations (which are modal adverbs) and their equivalents include:

inte, icke and **ej**, not

Ej is usually only found in written language: **ej upp**, not up, (on escalators).

Icke (not **inte**) is usually found in compounds: **en icke-kristen**, a non-Christian.

Knappast, knappt, scarcely

Han sa knappast någonting.   He scarcely said anything.

6 Compound adverbs are formed from an adverb + preposition (or adverb):

här (*adv.*) + **ifrån** (*prep*) → **härifrån**

Others include:

hemåt, norrut, hittills, härefter, därför, härmed, bortom, därvid

Other frequent compound adverbs are:

ännu, ändå, ibland, numera, omkring, häromdagen, nuförtiden

7 Comparative forms

Many adverbs compare like the adjectives from which they derive (see also 4.5.1 ff):

Positive	Comparative	Superlative	
tidigt	**tidigare**	**tidigast**	early, earlier, earliest
sent	**senare**	**senast**	late, later, latest
högt	**högre**	**högst**	high, higher, highest
långt	**längre**	**längst**	long, longer, longest (distance), far, further, furthest

Others include:

Positive	Comparative	Superlative	
länge	**längre**	**längst**	long, longer, longest (time)
väl	**bättre**	**bäst**	well, better, best
illa	**sämre**	**sämst**	badly, worse, worst
	värre	**värst**	See 4.5.7(2) for usage
mycket	**mer(a)**	**mest**	a lot, more, most
fort	**fortare**	**fortast**	quickly, more quickly, most quickly
gärna	**hellre**	**helst**	willingly, more willingly, most willingly
ofta	**oftare**	**oftast**	often, more often, most often
nära	**närmare**	**närmast**	close, closer, closest

8.2 **Use of adverbs**

1 Adverbs may qualify:

(a) A verb:	**Han sprang fort.**	He ran quickly.
(b) An adjective:	**Sjön var otroligt vacker.**	The lake was incredibly beautiful.
(c) An adverb:	**Hon sjöng ovanligt vackert.**	She sang unusually beautifully.
(d) A clause:	**Det blir troligen regn ikväll.**	It will probably rain tonight.

2 Amplifiers

(a) These are adverbs that qualify an adjective or another adverb, especially one denoting degree or kind. They include:

mycket (very), **helt** (completely), **alldeles** (completely), **ganska** (quite), **lagom** (suitably), **rätt** (very), **för** (too), **lite** (a little), **inte alls** (not at all), **bra** (very)

Det var en mycket intressant film.
It was a very interesting film.

Det gick inte alls bra.
It didn't go at all well.

(b) **Mycket** = 'very' when qualifying an adjective in the positive or an adverb:

Han var mycket lång.	He was very tall.
De gick mycket fort.	They walked very fast.

Mycket = 'much, a lot' when qualifying an adjective in the comparative or a verb:

Han var mycket längre än sin bror.
He was much taller than his brother.

Han sjöng mycket på den tiden.
He sang a lot in those days.

Cf. Väldigt mycket . . . = 'very much . . .'

Han är väldigt mycket rikare än alla sina bröder.
He is very much richer than all his brothers.

(c) Inte särskilt . . . = 'not very . . .'

Han är inte särskilt rik.　　　　He is not very rich.

Cf. Inte mycket . . . = 'not much . . .'

Han är inte mycket rikare än sin bror.
He isn't much richer than his brother.

(d) Sometimes adverbs formed from adjectives (see 8.1) are used as amplifiers:

Det blev förskräckligt varmt.　　It became awfully hot.

Jag har hemskt bråttom.　　　　I am in a terrible hurry.

Vi såg en fantastiskt bra match.　We saw a fantastically good
　　　　　　　　　　　　　　　　match.

8.3　Adverbs indicating location and motion

1 Adverbs express this distinction in Swedish which is now no longer found in English. One form is found with verbs indicating location at a place, another with verbs indicating motion towards a place and a third with verbs indicating motion away from a place:

Han bor här.	He lives here.	Location
Han kom hit.	He came here.	Motion towards
Han gick härifrån.	He left here.	Motion away from

English used to have this distinction in 'here/hither/hence', 'there/thither/thence'.

Location Where?		Motion towards Where to?		Motion away from Where from?	
var(?)	where	**vart**(?)	where (to)	**varifrån**(?)	where from
här	here	**hit**	(to) here	**härifrån**	from here
där	there	**dit**	(to) there	**därifrån**	from there
inne	in(side)	**in**	in	**inifrån**	from inside
ute	out(side)	**ut**	out	**utifrån**	from outside
uppe	up	**upp**	up	**uppifrån**	from above
nere	down	**ner**	down	**nerifrån**	from below
hemma	(at) home	**hem**	(to) home	**hemifrån**	from home
borta	away	**bort**	away	**bortifrån**	from that direction
framme	forward	**fram**	forward	**framifrån**	from the front

Notice the following idiomatic usages:

Jag ringde dit igår.	I rang there yesterday.
Vi längtar hem.	We long for home.
Han bor tre trappor upp.	He lives on the third floor. (US Eng. fourth floor)
Han satt längst bort.	He sat furthest away.
Cf. **När är vi framme?/** **När kommer vi fram?**	When will we get there?

2 How to translate 'where':

	Location	Motion
Interrogative (V-word)	**var**	**vart**
	Var är han? Where is he?	**Vart går han?** Where is he going?
Relative	**där**	**dit**
	Jag vet ett kafé där vi kan äta.	**Jag vet ett kafé dit vi kan gå.**
	I know a café where we can eat.	I know a café where we can go.

The relative adverb **där/dit** follows a noun or noun phrase:

Jag vet ett kafé där vi kan äta.

But

Jag vet var vi kan äta.

It is generally possible to replace **där/dit** by **som** + preposition when it is used in this way:

Jag vet ett kafé som vi kan äta på.
Jag vet ett kafé som vi kan gå till.

8.4   Some difficult adverbs

1   Då/sedan

(a) As an adverb **då** = 'then', 'at that moment/time', 'in that case':

Det blixtrade. Då började han springa.
There was a flash of lightning. Then he began to run.

Är du vaken? Då bör du stiga upp.
Are you awake? Then you had better get up.

Note: **Då** can also be:

(i) a temporal conjunction = 'when' (see 11.2(2)):

Då vi kom hem åt vi frukost.
When we got home we ate breakfast.

(ii) a causal conjunction = 'as' (see 11.4(2)):

Då jag hade pengar köpte jag en bil.
As I had money I bought a car.

(b) As an adverb **sedan** = 'then', 'after that', 'subsequently':

Först klippte vi gräsmattan. Sedan rensade vi ogräs.
First we cut the lawn. Then we weeded.

Note: **Sedan** can also be:

(i) a temporal conjunction = 'after', 'since' (see 11.2(2)):

Sedan han for är hon inte sig lik.   Since he left she has not been herself.

(ii) a preposition = 'since':

Jag har känt honom sedan kriget.   I have known him since the war.

2   Därför/därför att

(a) **Därför** is an adverb = 'for this reason', 'consequently', 'that is why', 'which is why':

Det är varmt. Därför svettas jag.
It's hot. That's why I'm sweating.

(b) **Därför att** is a subordinating conjunction = 'because', 'on account of', 'owing to':

Varför svettas du? (Jag svettas) Därför att det är varmt.
Why are you sweating? (I'm sweating) Because it's hot.

3 Eller hur?

Like French 'n'est-ce pas?', German 'nicht wahr?' this phrase concludes a sentence, corresponding to the English tag-question:

Han har fått sina pengar, eller hur?
He has got his money, hasn't he?

Han kommer hem idag, eller hur?
He's coming home today, isn't he?

The phrase is rapidly being replaced by **va?** (derived from **vad**) as a tag question:

Vi tittar på teve, va?　　We'll watch TV, shall we?

4 Först

(a) = 'first' (in time expressions):

Jag följer med, men först　　I'll come, but first I have to
måste jag byta om.　　　change.

(b) = 'not until, only':

Först igår fick jag veta det.　It was only yesterday that I found out.

Jag kom hem först igår.　　I didn't get home until yesterday.

5 Gärna

(a) = 'willingly', 'with pleasure', 'by all means':

Dricker du kaffe?　　　Do you drink coffee?
Ja, gärna.　　　　　　Yes, by all means.

(b) = 'like to':

Han badar gärna.　　　He likes to swim.

Note: **Hellre** and **helst**, the comparative and superlative forms of **gärna**, correspond to 'prefer(s) ... to ...', 'rather' and 'preferably', 'most of all' respectively:

Han dricker hellre öl än vin.　He prefers beer to wine.

Te eller kaffe? Hellre kaffe, tack. Tea or coffee? I'd rather have coffee, please.

När vill du åka? Helst idag.　When do you want to go? Today, preferably.

(c) = 'certainly':

Han får gärna försöka.　　He can certainly try.

149

6 Långt/länge

(a) **Långt** = 'far' (distance):

Hur långt är det till stan?   How far is it to town?

(b) **Länge** = 'long' (time):

Hur länge har du bott   How long have you lived
i Sverige?   in Sweden?

Notice, however, that the adjective in time expressions like those below is always **lång**:

Hur lång tid tar det?   How long will it take?

7 Ju, nog, väl, nämligen

As unstressed modal adverbs these words indicate the speaker's attitude to the utterance. When stressed, however, **nog** = 'enough', **väl** = 'well', 'rather'.

(a) **Ju** = 'you know', 'of course', 'to be sure', 'it is true'. You expect the listener to agree.

Det har jag ju aldrig sagt.   I've never said that, you know.

Du har ju varit här förr.   You've been here before, of course.

(b) **Nog** = 'probably', 'presumably', 'I expect', 'I daresay'. The speaker injects a note of doubt or conciliation.

Han kommer nog imorgon.   He'll be here tomorrow, I expect.

Hon klarar det nog.   She'll manage it all right.

(c) **Väl** = 'surely', 'I hope', 'I suppose'. The speaker hopes the listener will agree.

Du är väl inte sjuk?   You are not ill, surely?

Du kommer väl?   You'll be coming, I hope?

(d) **Nämligen** = 'you understand', 'you see'. New information is provided.

Du måste komma idag. Imorgon är jag nämligen i Uppsala.
You'll have to come today. Tomorrow, you see, I'll be in Uppsala.

Cf. **Du måste komma idag. Imorgon är jag ju i Uppsala.**

You'll have to come today. Tomorrow, as you know, I'll be in Uppsala.

8 Redan

(a) = 'already':

Är du färdig redan?
Have you finished already?

(b) = 'even':

Redan en ytlig undersökning visade detta.
Even a superficial investigation revealed this.

(c) = 'as early as':

Redan på 1600-talet var Sverige en stormakt.
As early as in the 17th century Sweden was a great power.

Chapter 9

Interjections

9.1 Interjections

Interjections are not inflected. They almost invariably come first in the sentence or clause, and are usually marked off by a comma.

1 Ja, nej, jo, etc.

(a) In answer to a positive yes/no question **ja/nej** is used:

Tänker du gå på bio? Ja/Nej.
Are you thinking of going to the cinema? Yes/No.

Strong agreement is indicated by **javisst** or **jovisst**; surprise or disinterest by **jaså!**

(b) If the question assumes a negative answer and the answer stresses a positive response, then **jo** is used:

Du tänker väl inte gå på bio? Jo!
You're not thinking of going to the cinema, are you? Yes, I am!

2 Expressions of feeling, exclamations

Pain:	**aj, o, puh**	**Aj, vad det gör ont!**	Ow, that hurts!
Surprise:	**oj, o, å**	**Oj, vad vackert!**	Oh, how beautiful!
Disgust:	**usch, fy, hu**	**Usch, vad hemskt!**	Ugh, how horrible!

3 Commands

Kusch, Hut = Down! (to dogs), **Ptro** = Whoah (to horses), **Hyssch** = Shhh (to children), **Giv akt!** = Attention! (to soldiers)

4 Imitations

Sounds made by animals:

vov vov (woof), **miau** (miaou), **bää** (baa)

Sounds made by objects:

pang (bang), **plask** (splash), **bing-bång** (ding-dong)

5 Greetings, exhortations

(a) Meeting, parting:

Goddag! (How do you do?), **Välkommen!** (plural: **Välkomna!**)
(Welcome), **Adjö!** (formal: Goodbye), **Hej då!** (Bye bye), **Vi ses!**
(Be seeing you), **Hej!** (Hallo), **Hejsan!** (Hi there!)

(b) Good wishes, thanks:

Skål! (Cheers), **Gott nytt år!** (Happy New Year), **Varsågod!** (plural:
Varsågoda!) (Here you are/You're welcome), **Tack** (Thanks/Cheers),
Tack så mycket! (Thank you), **Ha den ära(n)!** (Many happy
returns), **Gratulerar/Grattis!** (Congratulations), **Prosit!** (Bless you)

(c) Apologies, etc.:

Förlåt! (Sorry), **Ursäkta!** (Excuse me/Pardon me), **För all del!/Ingen
fara** (By all means/Don't mention it/No problem),
Hursa?/Vasa?/Förlåt (Pardon/Could you repeat that?)

6 Expletives:

**Sjutton! Kors! Herre Gud! Tusan! Förbaskat! Jösses! Fy
fasen! Jäklar! Skit! Helvete! Förbannat! Fy fan! Jävlar!
Jävlaranamma! Satan!**

Chapter 10

Prepositions

10.1 Prepositions – introduction

1 Prepositions are indeclinable words or set phrases, generally unstressed in speech except when standing after a verb as a stressed particle (7.5.18, 12.6.7).

2 Swedish prepositions have the following prepositional complements:

(a) a noun:

> **Han cyklar till staden.**   He's cycling to town.

(b) a pronoun in the object form:

> **Vi pratade med honom.**   We spoke to him.

(c) an infinitive phrase:

> **Han gick utan att vänta.**   He left without waiting.

(d) a subordinate clause:

> **Hon var säker på att hon hade rätt.**
> She was sure that she was right.

(e) a prepositional or adverbial phrase:

> **Vad gör vi efter idag?**
> What are we going to do after today?

> **Det håller jag för helt omöjligt.**
> I consider that totally impossible.

3 Prepositions may adopt three different positions relative to the complement:

(a) Before the complement (the majority of Swedish prepositions do this):

bakom **huset**	behind the house
framför **tvn**	in front of the TV
hos **Olssons**	at the Olssons'
i **augusti**	in August

(b) After the complement (few prepositions, called 'postpositions', do this; those that do are usually stressed):

året *om*	(all) year round
jorden *runt*	round the world
oss *emellan*	between you and me

(c) Bracketing the complement (called 'circumpositions'):

för **tio år** *sedan*	ten years ago
sedan **ett år** *tillbaka*	for the past year
för **din** *skull*	for your sake

4 Notice that in Swedish the preposition is correctly placed as the last element in a clause:

(a) in V-questions (see 5.11):

Vad tänker du på?	What are you thinking about?

(b) in relative clauses (see 12.8.1(2)):

Du är den (som) jag drömmer om.
You are the one of whom I dream.

(c) when the prepositional complement occupies the topic position (12.7.1):

Honom kan man inte lita på.	He's not to be relied on.

(d) in infinitive phrases:

Du är omöjlig att arbeta med.	You're impossible to work with.

(e) in exclamations:

Vilket stort hus du bor i!   What a big house you live in!

5   Some prepositions consist of adverb + preposition:

Han kom in i huset.   He came into the house.

De satt framför brasan.   They sat in front of the fire.

10.2   The most common Swedish prepositions

Here is a list of frequent Swedish prepositions. Examples of common ways
in which the ten most frequent prepositions (**av, från, för, i, med, om, på,
till, under, vid**) are used are given in sections 10.2.1–10.2.10. Many of
the remaining Swedish prepositions are used in much the same way as
their English equivalents.

av	of, with, by	**längs**	along
bakom	behind	**med**	with, by
bland	among	**mellan**	between
bredvid	beside	**mot**	to(wards), against
efter	after, for	**om**	(a)round, about, in
enligt	according to	**på**	on, in, for
framför	in front of	**sedan**	since
från	from	**till**	until, to, for
för	for, by, with, of	**trots**	in spite of
för . . . sedan	ago	**under**	under(neath), below,
före	before		during
genom	through, by	**ur**	out of
hos	at (the home of)	**utan**	without
i	in, on, for	**utanför**	outside
inom	within	**utom**	except (for)
inför	before	**vid**	by, around
kring/omkring	(a)round	**åt**	to(wards), for
		över	over, above, across

Notes:

1 efter

(a) **Efter** corresponds to English 'for' after a number of verbs, to suggest the object of a desire or search:

Jag längtar efter engelsk mat.	I long for English food.
Vi letar/ringer efter dem.	We're looking/phoning for them.

(b) **Stäng dörren efter dig!**   Close the door behind you!

2 **För ... sedan** brackets the complement:

Detta hände för 10 år sedan.	This happened ten years ago.

3 **Genom** is used with the infinitive to render the English 'by' + 'ing' form in expressions such as:

Han vann genom att fuska.	He won by cheating.

4 **Hos** corresponds to French 'chez', German 'bei' (= at the place of work/home of):

Vi bor hos Linds.	We're staying with the Linds.
Han är hos tandläkaren.	He's at the dentist's.

Note also:

Det står hos Freud.	That's in Freud('s works).

5 **Inför** suggests English 'before', often in a figurative sense:

Han stod inför domaren.	He stood before the judge.
Han ställs inför svårigheter.	He's faced with difficulties.
Jag var orolig inför resan.	I was uneasy before (= at the prospect of) the journey.

6 Åt

(a) renders 'to(wards)' in set expressions of place:

Åt vilket håll ska jag köra?	Which direction shall I drive in?
Kör åt vänster/åt norr.	Drive to the left/north!

(b) may indicate an indirect object and is then rendered in English by 'for':

Köp en åt mig också!	Buy one for me too!

7 Över

(a) corresponds also to English 'past' in clock-time expressions:

Klockan är fem minuter över två.	It's five past two.

(b) Note also:

en karta över Sverige	a map of Sweden
en lista över deltagarna	a list of participants

157

10.2.1 Av

Av basically suggests origin or source, although **från** is more common with origins that are actual locations. **Av** is also used to indicate the passive agent (see 7.5.17, 12.6.8, 12.7.6).

Agent by	Material of	Cause from/with	Location off/from	Measure of	Possession of
BY					
Huset köptes av en svensk.			The house was bought by a Swede.		
en film (skriven) av Bergman			A film (written) by Bergman		
OF					
Huset är byggt av tegel.			The house is built of brick.		
Det står i utkanten av stan.			It's on the edge of town.		
Kungen av Sverige			The King of Sweden		
Nio av tio svar var riktiga.			Nine out of ten answers were correct.		
Det var snällt/duktigt av dig.			That was kind/clever of you.		
FROM					
Jag får ont i huvudet av bullret.			I get a headache from the noise.		
Får du någon glädje av det?			Do you get pleasure from that?		
WITH					
Hon grät av rädsla/glädje.			She cried with fear/with joy.		
OFF					
Han steg/hoppade av bussen.			He got/jumped off the bus.		

Note also:

på grund av 'because of, due to'; **med hjälp av** 'with the aid of'; **av misstag** 'by mistake'; **av en händelse** 'by chance'

10.2.2 Från

Från (sometimes **ifrån**) is used much the same as English 'from' to suggest origin, a point of departure or vantage.

Location	Source	Time
from	*from*	*from*

FROM

Det står 220 meter från vägen.	It's 220 metres from the road.
När flyttade du från Sverige?	When did you move from Sweden?
Utifrån det vi vet . . .	From what we know . . .

Note:

A number of adverbial expressions of place are formed with post-positioned **ifrån** (see 8.3(1)):

Var kommer du ifrån?	Where do you come from?

10.2.3 För

För corresponds to English 'for' in a wide range of senses, but not generally with time expressions (see 10.3.2):

Intention/Purpose	Indirect object	Cause
for	*to*	*for*

FOR

ett program för barn	a programme for children
Jag gör det för dig/för din skull.	I do it for you/for your sake.
Tack för hjälpen!	Thanks for your help!
Han är känd/berömd för det.	He is renowned/famous for that.
Vad gråter du för?	What are you crying for?
en gång för alla	once and for all

TO

Förklara det för mig!	Explain it to me!
Kan jag vara till hjälp för dig?	Can I be of help to you?
Tala om för oss vad som hände.	Tell us what happened.
Han berättade historien för mig.	He told me the story.

Note also:

Jag är rädd för ormar.	I'm afraid of snakes.
Han intresserar sig för musik.	He's interested in music.
Jag har svårt/lätt för språk.	I find languages hard/easy.
att skriva för hand	to write by hand
dag för dag	day by day
för det första/andra osv	in the first/second place, etc.
Vad är det för slags bil?	What kind of car is it?

159

10.2.4 **i**

I is the second most frequent word in Swedish, with many idiomatic usages beyond its basic meaning 'in'. With public buildings and places of work or entertainment, English 'in' is often rendered by Swedish **på** (see 10.2.7, 10.3.4). For the uses of **i** with expressions of time, see 10.3.2.

Location in/on/at	Material in	Time when in	Time duration for	State in	Frequency per

IN

Han sitter i rummet.	He is sitting in the room.
en staty i brons	a statue in bronze
Han är i god form.	He's in good shape.
De kommer i april.	They're coming in April.

ON

Hon sitter i gräset/soffan.	She's sitting on the grass/ sofa.

AT

Mor är i kyrkan.	Mother's at church.

FOR

De stannade i fem veckor.	They stayed for five weeks.

PER

90 kilometer i timmen	90 kilometres per hour
en gång i veckan/i månaden	once a week/a month

Note also:

Går Eva i skolan/i kyrkan?	Does Eva go to school/to church?
Klockan är fem minuter i tio.	It's five minutes to ten.
Jag har ont i magen/huvudet.	I have a stomach-ache/headache.
Han tvättar sig i ansiktet.	He washes his face. (See also 3.6.5.)

10.2.5 Med

Med may be used to render most of the meanings of English 'with'.

Manner *by/with/in*	Possession *with*
WITH	
Han åkte dit med sin familj.	He went there with his family.
Han är mannen med sex söner.	He's the man with six sons.
Hur står det till med dig?	How are things with you?
Ät inte med fingrarna!	Don't eat with your fingers!
Det värsta med honom är hans dåliga humör.	The worst thing with (= about) him is his bad temper.
kaffe med grädde	coffee with cream
BY	
åka med buss/bil/tåg osv	travel by bus/car/train, etc.
Skicka pengarna med posten!	Send the money by post.
IN	
Tala med hög röst!	Speak in a loud voice!
Note also:	
Får jag prata med honom?	May I speak to him?
ha dåligt med tid/pengar osv	to have little time/money, etc.
Jag har inte tid med det.	I've no time for that.

| 10.2.6 | Om |

Om is used in a great many idiomatic senses, perhaps most frequently in certain expressions indicating future time (see 10.3.2).

Location (a)round	Future time when in	Subject matter on/about
(A)ROUND		
Ta en halsduk om halsen!	Put a scarf round your neck.	
IN		
De kommer om en vecka.	They're coming in a week('s time).	
ABOUT/ON		
Vi har pratat om dig.	We have been talking about you.	
en bok om Sverige	a book about/on Sweden	
Det är synd om honom.	It's a pity about him.	
Note also:		
norr om/söder om	north of/south of	
gott om/ont om	plenty of/little (= a lack of)	
tycka synd om	to feel sorry for someone	
tre gånger om dagen/året	three times a day/year	

In certain instances, primarily with parts of the body, **om** is used without an English equivalent (see also 3.6.5):

Han är smutsig/kall/våt/om händerna.
His hands are dirty/cold/wet.

| **Jag fryser om tårna.** | My toes are cold. |
| **Du är röd om kinderna.** | Your cheeks are red. |

| 10.2.7 | På |

På is used in many idiomatic senses in addition to the basic meaning of 'on (top of)'. **På** is often used to render English 'in' with public buildings and places of work or entertainment (see 10.3.4). For uses of **på** with expressions of time, see 10.3.2.

Location on/at/in	Motion to	Time when on + days in + season at + festival	Time duration in, not … for … (see 10.3.2(4))	Measure of	Possession of

---

ON

Det ligger på bordet.	It's on the table.
Han satte hatten på huvudet.	He put his hat on his head.
Vi åker dit på söndagarna.	We go there on Sundays.

IN

Jag arbetar på en bank/ett hotell.	I work in a bank/a hotel.
Vi åker dit på vintern.	We go there in winter.
Han gör allt på väldigt kort tid.	He does everything in a very short time.

NOT … FOR

Jag har inte träffat henne på länge.	I've not seen her for a long time.

AT

Vi träffades på biblioteket/bion.	We met at the library/cinema.
Vad gör ni på julen?	What are you doing at Christmas?

TO

Vi går på bio/matchen.	We're going to the cinema/match.

OF

ett barn på fyra år	a child of four
titeln på/priset på boken	the title/price of the book
i början på augusti	at the beginning of August

Note also:

Jag tänker ofta på dig.	I often think of you.
Vi väntar på dig.	We're waiting for you.
på samma sätt/på detta sätt	in the same way/in this way
Han är bra/dålig på att simma.	He is good/bad at swimming.

10.2.8 Till

Basically **till** suggests movement or progression towards some target, but it may also be used to express indirect object relationships.

Motion to	Time when until	Indirect object to/for	Possession of
TO			
Han reser till Amerika.	He's going to America.		
Han kom till makten 1929.	He came to power in 1929.		
ett nio till fem jobb	a nine-to-five job		
Vad sa han till de andra?	What did he say to the others?		
UNTIL			
Kan du stanna till imorgon?	Can you stay until tomorrow?		
FOR			
Vi åt fisk till lunch.	We had fish for lunch.		
Han köpte en bil till mig.	He bought a car for me.		
Vad använder du det till?	What do you use that for?		
till exempel	for example		
OF			
Nils är en gammal vän till mig.	Nils is an old friend of mine.		

Note also:

Han är elektriker till yrket.	He is an electrician by trade.

10.2.9 Under

Basically **under** corresponds to ideas expressed by English 'below', 'under(neath)', etc. However, it is also used to render English 'during'.

Location *under/below/beneath*	Time duration *during/for*	Measure *under/below*
UNDER		
Boken ligger under bordet.	The book is under the table.	
Bilen körde under bron.	The car drove under the bridge.	
barn under femton (år)	children under 15 (years old)	
Är allt under kontroll?	Is everything under control?	
BELOW		
vid temperaturer under noll	at temperatures below zero	
DURING		
Vad gjorde du under kriget?	What did you do during the war?	
Vi blev goda vänner under samtalets gång.	We became firm friends during the course of the conversation.	

| 10.2.10 | Vid |

Vid suggests adjacency or proximity.

Location *by/at*	Time when *around*
BY	
Vi har en stuga vid kusten.	We have a cottage by/on the coast.
Han satt vid fönstret.	He sat by the window.
AT	
Han satt vid bordet.	He sat at the table.
Hon studerar vid universitetet.	She's studying at university.
AROUND	
Vi träffas vid tiotiden.	We'll meet around ten.
Note also:	
vid ankomst/vid avgång	on arrival/on departure
vid närmare eftertanke	on closer consideration
en man vid namn Jansson	a man called Jansson
Han är fortfarande vid liv.	He's still alive.

| 10.3 | **Translating prepositions** |

| 10.3.1 | *Some common English prepositions and their Swedish equivalents* |

Before attempting to render English prepositional phrases into Swedish, consult the table below for help in choosing a suitable Swedish equivalent.

	Time	Place	Manner	Subject matter	Indirect object	Agent	Measure
about	**omkring/ vid**	**omkring**		**om**			**omkring**
above		**över**					**över/ framför**
after	**efter**	**efter/ bakom**	**efter**				
against		**mot**	**mot**				
at	10.3.2(3)	10.3.4					
before	**före**	**framför/ före**					
below	**under**	**under**					
by	**före/till**	**vid/hos**	**med/ genom**			**av**	
during	**under**						
for	10.3.2(4)				**för/att/till**		**till/för**
from	**från**	**från/av**					
in	10.3.2(1)	10.3.4 **i/på**					
into		**in i**					
of				10.3.5			10.2.1, 10.3.5
on	10.3.2(2)	10.3.4		**om**			
over	**över**	**över**					**över**
through	**under/ genom**	**genom**	**genom**				
to	**till/ i** + clock time	10.2(6) 10.2.4, 10.2.7			**till/för**		
under		**under**	**under**				
with		**hos**	**med**				

Translating 'in, on, at', etc., as expressions of time

Because of the idiomatic nature of Swedish prepositional expressions of time, it is difficult to formulate rules which are both concise and 100 per cent reliable. For the sake of brevity some variations have been deliberately omitted from what follows. The aim here is to indicate a scheme of basic conventions applicable in the majority of instances.

1 'in' + expressions of time

In +	Year	Decade/Century	Month	Season
past	⊗år 1949	på 1800-talet	i januari	i våras/på våren
habitual	–	–	i januari	på våren
present	–	–	i januari	i vår
future	⊗år 2030	på 2200-talet	i januari	i vår

Notes:

1 The preposition **om** (Eng. 'in') answers the question 'When?' to express future action:

De reser om en timme/om en vecka/om ett par år.
They're going in an hour/in a week/in a couple of years.

2 The preposition **på** (Eng. 'in') answers the question 'How long does it/will it take?':

De reser dit på en timme/på en vecka.
They can travel there in an hour/in a week.
i.e. It will take them an hour/a week to get there.

3 **I våras**, etc. and **i vår**, etc., both render English 'in spring', etc., but mean 'last spring' and 'next spring' respectively.

4 For less specific expressions with seasons **på våren** is used for both past and future:

Detta hände på våren för länge sedan.
This happened in the spring many years ago.

5 The preposition **på** is usually omitted when the season is followed by a year date:

Detta hände våren 1986 och kommer att hända igen våren 2062.
This happened in the spring of 1986 and will happen again in the spring of 2062.

6 Note the idiomatic use of **på** to render 'in/for' as an expression indicating duration in negative sentences (see also 4 'for + duration' below):

Jag har inte sett henne på tre år/på länge.
I haven't seen her for three years/for a long time.

2 'on' + expressions of time

On +	Weekday	Date
past	**i söndags**	**den 1:a (första) juli**
habitual	**på söndagarna**	**den 1:a (första) juli**
present	**(idag)**	**den 1:a (första) juli**
future	**på söndag**	**den 1:a (första) juli**

Notes:

1 **I söndags**, etc., and **på söndag**, etc., render English 'on Sunday' = 'last Sunday', etc. and 'this/next Sunday', etc., respectively.

2 For less specific expressions of time **(på) en söndag**, etc., may be used.

Detta hände (på) en söndag för länge sedan.
This happened on a Sunday/one Sunday a long time ago.

3 For weekday + calendar date expressions Swedish usually has the definite form of the weekday and no preposition:

Detta hände fredagen den 1:a mars och händer igen söndagen den 5:e maj.
This happened on Friday March 1st and will happen again on Sunday May 5th.

4 **I söndags**, etc., may be combined with the parts of the day:

Detta hände i söndags morse.
This happened on Sunday morning.

3 'at' + expressions of time

At +	Festival	Clock
past	**i julas**	**klockan 10 (tio)**
habitual	**på jul/på jularna**	**klockan 10 (tio)**
present	**i jul**	**klockan 10 (tio)**
future	**i jul/till jul**	**klockan 10 (tio)**

Notes:

1 **I julas**, etc., and **i jul**, etc., render English 'at Christmas' = 'last Christmas', etc. and 'this/next Christmas', etc., respectively.

2 For less specific expressions of time **på julen**, etc., may be used.

Detta hände på julen för många år sedan.
This happened at Christmas many years ago.

3 With year-date expressions Swedish usually has the definite form of the festival and no preposition:

Detta hände julen 1954 och kommer att hända igen julen 2027.
This happened at Christmas 1954 and will happen again at Christmas 2027.

4 'for' + duration

Swedish **i** + expression of time:

Han har bott här i tre år.
He's lived here for three years.

Swedish **under** if English 'for' = 'for the duration of':

Han bodde här under kriget.
He lived here for the war.

Swedish **på** renders English 'for/in' in negative clauses:

Jag har inte bott där på 5 år.
I haven't lived there for/in five years.

Note also:

for a long time	**länge** (no preposition!)
not for a long time	**inte ... på länge**

10.3.3 *Prepositions in expressions of time – summary*

	Past	Habitual	Present	Future
Seasons	**förra våren/ i våras** last spring	**på våren** in (the) spring	**i vår** this spring	**i vår/nästa vår** next spring
Festivals	**förra julen/ i julas** last Xmas	**på julen på jularna** at Xmas	**i jul** this Xmas	**i jul/nästa jul** next Xmas
Days	**igår** yesterday	**varje dag** every day	**i dag** today	**i morgon** tomorrow
	i söndags last Sunday	**på söndagarna** on Sundays		**på söndag** next Sunday
Parts of the day	**i morse** (earlier) this morning	**på morgonen/ morgnarna** in the morning/s	**nu på morgonen** this morning	**imorgon bitti** tomorrow morning
	i eftermiddags (earlier) this afternoon	**på efter- middagen** in the afternoon	**nu på efter- middagen** this afternoon	**i eftermiddag** (later) this afternoon

	igår kväll	på kvällen/ kvällarna	ikväll	imorgon kväll
	last night	in the evening/s	this evening	tomorrow evening
	i natt	**på natten/ nätterna**	**i natt**	**i natt**
	last night/ during the night	at night	tonight	(later) tonight
Years, months	**i fjol/förra året**	**varje år**	**i år**	**nästa år**
	last year	every year	this year	next year
	i januari	**i januari**	**i januari**	**i januari**
	last January	in January	this January	next January

10.3.4 | Translating 'in, on, at', etc., as expressions of place

Because of the idiomatic usages of **i** and **på**, translation of 'in', 'on', 'at', etc., expressing place relationships is not always straightforward. A rule of thumb (to which there are many exceptions!) is that Swedish usage requires:

på + surface	*i* + volume
tavlan på väggen	**möss i väggen**
the picture on the wall	mice in the wall
duken på bordet	**duken i lådan**
the cloth on the table	the cloth in the drawer
en sajt på webben	**ett fel i datorn**
a site on the internet	a fault in the computer
Note: **Han bor på landet.**	**Han bor i landet.**
He lives in the country(side).	He lives in the country (i.e. state).
	prata i telefon
	speak on the telephone
	ett program i radio/TV
	a programme on the radio/TV
Han sitter på en stol.	**Han sitter i en stol.**
He's sitting on a (dining) chair.	He's sitting in an armchair.

Major exceptions:

1 **På** = 'in'/'at' with public buildings, etc.

   Vi träffades på museet/IKEA/sjukhuset/hotellet.
   We met in the museum/in IKEA/in the hospital/at the hotel.

2 **På** = 'in'/'at' with place of work or study:

   Hon är på jobbet/på ett möte.   She's at work/in a meeting.

   Han arbetar på Volvo/på ett fik.   He works at Volvo/in a café.

3 **På** = 'in'/'at'/'on' with places of entertainment or enjoyment:

   Vi träffades på en dans/på bion/på ett bröllop/på semester.
   We met at a dance/at the cinema/at a wedding/on holiday.

4 **Hos** = 'at' with the names of people or their professions to indicate 'at the place of work/home of':

   Vi var hos Olssons.   We were at the Olssons' (place).

   Han är hos frisören.   He's at the hairdresser's.

5 **Vid** = 'on'/'at'/'by' with many words for things which extend lengthwise:

   Han bor vid kusten.   He lives on the coast.

   Han stod vid disken/floden.   He stood at the counter/by the river.

10.3.5 *Translating 'of'*

The English preposition 'of' may be rendered in a great many ways in Swedish. What follows provides hints on how to translate 'of' in some common instances:

1 Possessive 'of'

(a) English possessive 'of' is commonly rendered by Swedish s-genitives (cf. 3.7.1):

   the meaning of life   **livets mening**
   the title of the book   **bokens titel**

(b) In many cases Swedish prefers a compound noun:

   the tops of the mountains   **fjälltopparna**
   (cf. the mountain tops)

   the leg of the table (cf. the table leg)   **bordsbenet**

(c) Double genitives (English: 'of' + possessive adjective/s-genitive noun) are generally constructed with **till** + possessive pronoun/noun in Swedish (cf. 10.2.8):

   a friend of yours/the president's   **en vän till dig/presidenten**

2 Appositive genitive

When English 'of' may be replaced by commas indicating apposition, it is rendered without a preposition in Swedish:

the kingdom of Norway	**kungariket Norge**
(the kingdom, Norway)	
the month of May	**månaden maj**

Note:

The city of Stockholm (= urban area)	**staden Stockholm**
The City of Stockholm (= municipal council)	**Stockholms stad**
the battle of Lützen	**slaget vid Lützen**

3 Partitive genitive

Expressions with 'of' indicating measure are generally rendered without a preposition in Swedish:

a cup of tea	**en kopp te**
a pair of shoes	**ett par skor**
12 kilos of peas	**12 kilo ärter**
a large number of Swedes	**ett stort antal svenskar**

Notes:

1 Half of/part of the book   **hälften av/en del av boken**

2 Swedish usually has **på** when English 'of' is followed by a number:

a boy of 5	**en pojke på 5 år**
a monthly wage of 25,000 kronor	**en månadslön på 25000 kronor**

4 Dates

Swedish usually has no preposition for 'of' used in dates:

the first of January	**den 1:a (första) januari**
in May of 1956	**i maj 1956**

5 'A heart of stone' etc.

'Of' indicating material is rendered by **av** in Swedish (cf. 10.2.1):

a heart of stone	**ett hjärta av sten**
a statue of gold	**en staty av guld**

173

6 'The king of Sweden', etc.

'Of' indicating origin is generally rendered by Swedish **av**:

the king of Sweden	**kungen av Sverige**

7 'North of' etc.

'Of' in locations and directions expressed by compass points or 'left'/'right' is rendered by **om** in Swedish:

north of Malmö	**norr om Malmö**
left of the church	**till vänster om kyrkan**

Note:

the north of England/Sweden	**norra England/Sverige**

Chapter 11

Conjunctions

11.1 Coordinating conjunctions

These join clauses or elements of the same kind and are always found between the words or groups of words that they link (see 12.4). They do *not* affect the word order within the groups of words that they link.

Coordination (linking) of:

two subjects	*Hans* **och** *Greta* **lyssnar på jazz.**
two verbs	**De** *sitter* **och** *lyssnar.*
two main clauses (straight word order)	*Jag tycker om Olle* **och** *han älskar mig.*
two main clauses (inverted word order)	*Popmusik älskar jag,* **och** *det gör hon också.*
two subordinate clauses	**Jag hoppas** *att han vinner* **och** *att han har rekordtid.*

Coordinating conjunctions include:

och/samt	and	**Möblerna och tavlorna såldes.**
eller	or	**Pengar eller livet!**
men	but	**Han är smart men ful.** See Note 2 below, 11.4(6).
utan	but	**Han var inte full utan bara trött.** See 11.4(6).
fast	but, (al)though	**Mor var sjuk, fast det kunde jag ju inte veta.**
för	as, because	**Han kom inte för han var sjuk.**
så	so	**Det är sent, så vi går nu.**
som	as	**Då som nu var det stor arbetslöshet här.**
plus	and, as well as	**Vi köpte hela köket och badrummet plus en del möbler.**

Notes:

1 **Och** links elements of equal weight, whereas **samt** links elements of unequal weight:

> **Kansliet samt biblioteket hålls stängda under sommaren.**
> (**Kansliet** is more important.)
> The offices and library are closed during the summer.

2 **Utan** replaces **men** after a negative when the second element contradicts the first:

> **Han köpte inte bilen utan stal den.**   He did not buy the car, but stole it.

Other constructions include:

både . . . och	partly . . . partly, both . . . and
såväl . . . som	both . . . and
inte bara . . . utan också	not only . . . but also
antingen . . . eller	either . . . or
varken . . . eller	neither . . . nor

11.2   Subordinating conjunctions

These link main clauses to subordinate clauses, and always introduce the subordinate clause wherever it is positioned in the sentence. Some subordinating conjunctions may therefore begin the sentence:

Jag sover MC	*när* **jag är trött.** sub conj + SC	I sleep when I'm tired.
När **jag är trött** sub conj + SC	**sover jag.** MC	When I'm tired I sleep.

Some Swedish subordinating conjunctions never introduce a sentence, however:

Hon kom hit	*för att* **hon ville lära sig svenska.** sub conj + SC
She came here	(in order) to learn Swedish.

Subordinating conjunctions and other words (see 11.3) which introduce subordinate clauses do affect the word order and occupy the first position in the subordinate clause (see 12.8.2). There are two main types of subordinating conjunction:

1 *General subordinators* introduce indirect speech (**att**) and indirect yes/no questions (**om**), but impart no meaning to the clause, unlike other subordinating conjunctions in 2 below:

	att	**Han sa *att* han arbetade hårt.**	that
cf.		**Jag arbetar hårt.**	
	om	**Jag undrar, *om* han arbetar så mycket.**	whether, if
cf.		**Arbetar han så mycket?**	

2 *Other subordinating conjunctions* introduce different kinds of adverbial clause (cf. 12.6.5):

(a) Time:

***När/Då/Sedan* han hade parkerat bilen, gick han in.**	when, after
***Medan* gräset gror, dör kon.**	while
***Innan* vi gick hem tackade vi värdinnan.**	before

(b) Cause:

Vi vann *därför att* vi var bäst.	because
***Eftersom/Sedan* de var sämre, förlorade de.**	since, as, because

(c) Condition:

***Om/Ifall* du är snäll ska du få glass.**	if

(d) Concession:

Han är glad *fast*(*än*) han inte är kry.	although

(e) Intention:

Vi måste friställa folk *för att* vi ska rädda firman.	in order that
Han skrev upp det *så* (*att*) han skulle minnas det.	so that
Se upp *så* (*att*) du inte blir överkörd!	so that

(f) Result:

Han sprang *så* fort *att* han blev andfådd.	so (. . . that)

(g) Comparison:

Han är *lika* stor *som* hans bror.	as . . . as . . .
Du är inte *så* gammal *som* jag.	as . . . as . . .
Hon var äldre *än* jag väntat mig.	than
***Ju* äldre jag blir *desto* tröttare blir jag.**	the . . . the . . .

11.3 Other subordinators

These are words which are not conjunctions, but nevertheless introduce subordinate clauses.

1 *Interrogative pronouns* (v-words) and *adverbs* (cf. 5.11)

These words introduce indirect v-questions (cf. 12.2(2), 12.3):

Jag undrade *vart* han hade tagit vägen.	where
cf. **Vart har han tagit vägen?**	
Jag undrar *vem som* kysser henne nu.	who
Jag vet inte *vilken* du menar.	which

2 *Relative pronouns* and *adverbs* (cf. 5.10)

These words introduce relative clauses (cf. 12.8.1(2)), which usually form attributes to subjects, objects or complements:

Brevet *som* jag skickade var handskrivet.   which, that
The letter (that) I sent was handwritten.

En man *vars* namn jag har glömt kom fram till mig.   whose
A man whose name I have forgotten came up to me.

Han hittade en skog *där* det fanns lingon.   where
He found a forest where there were lingonberries.

Gustav II Adolf blev med tiden tämligen fet, *vilket* alltid nämns i skolböckerna.
Gustavus Adolphus in time became rather fat, which is always mentioned in the textbooks.

11.4 Some problem conjunctions

1 'After' = both preposition and conjunction in English. **Efter** is only a preposition and cannot alone introduce a clause. **Efter** (**det**) **att** is used instead.

The house burned down shortly after they left.
Huset brann ner kort *efter* (det) att de åkte.

2 'As' = 'for' = **för**

He disappeared as he was afraid.
Han försvann *för* han var rädd.

'As' = 'while' = medan

As he was speaking he went red.
***Medan* han talade rodnade han.**

'As' = 'because' = eftersom/då

As he isn't coming we will begin.
***Eftersom* han inte kommer börjar vi.**

'As' = 'like' = (lik)som

Now as before it is very difficult.
Nu *liksom* förr är det mycket svårt.

3 'As . . . as . . .'

- when a comparison is made in a positive clause = lika . . . som

  He is as gifted as your sister.
  Han är *lika* begåvad *som* din syster.

- when a comparison is made in a negative clause = så . . . som

  He is not as gifted as you.   **Han är *inte så* begåvad *som* du.**

4 'Before'

- as a conjunction after a positive main clause = innan

  We visited him before we came here.
  Vi hälsade på honom *innan* vi kom hit.

- as a conjunction after a negative main clause = förrän

  It was not long before he arrived.
  Det dröjde inte länge *förrän* han kom.

- as an adverb = 'earlier', 'previously' = förr/förut/tidigare

  I have never been to Dalarna before.
  Jag har aldrig varit i Dalarna *förr/förut/tidigare*.

- as a preposition = **före/innan**

  We met Jan before Easter.   **Vi träffade Jan *före/innan* påsk.**

5 'Both'

- as a conjunction – 'both X and Y' = **både . . . och . . .**

  Both Erik and Eva were language students.
  ***Både* Erik *och* Eva var språkstuderande.**

- as an indefinite pronoun – 'both Xs' = **båda** (+ noun with end article)

  Both students studied languages.
  ***Båda* studenterna studerade språk.**

6 'But'

- as a conjunction after a positive clause or a negative clause not directly contradicting the first clause (i.e. *but in spite of that*) = **men**

  The essay is long but it does not say very much.
  Uppsatsen är lång *men* den säger inte mycket.

  The essay is not long but it is very boring.
  Uppsatsen är inte lång *men* den är mycket tråkig.

- as a conjunction after a negative main clause, when the second clause directly contradicts the first (i.e. *but on the contrary*) = **utan**

  The essay isn't long but is actually quite short.
  Uppsatsen är inte lång *utan* egentligen ganska kort.

Note also:

inte bara . . . utan också . . .

> **Hon var *inte bara* vacker *utan också* intelligent.**
> She was not only beautiful but also intelligent.

- as a preposition = **utom**

  All students but one have passed.
  Alla studenter *utom* en har blivit godkända.

7 'That'

- as a subordinating conjunction = **att**

  They said (that) they were pleased.
  De sa (*att*) de var nöjda.

- as a relative pronoun (= 'which', 'whom') = **som**

  Buy a house (that) you like.
  Köp ett hus (*som*) du tycker om!

- in cleft sentences (cf. 12.7.8) = **som**

  It was my idea that won the prize.
  Det var min idé *som* vann priset.

- in the expression 'now that' = **nu då/när**

  Now that she is here we can begin.
  ***Nu då* hon är här kan vi börja.**

Chapter 12

Word order and sentence structure

12.1 Word classes and sentence elements

Hitherto in this book we have examined word classes (or parts of speech), i.e. words grouped according to their form or meaning, e.g. nouns, verbs. In this section of the book we examine sentence elements, i.e. the function of words and groups of words in the sentence.

	Vi	har	inte	köpt	tidningen	ikväll
	We	have	not	bought	the paper	tonight
Word class	*Pronoun*	*Verb*	*Adverb*	*Verb*	*Noun*	*Adverb*
Sentence Element	*Subject*	*Finite verb*	*Clausal adverbial*	*Non-finite verb*	*Object*	*Other adverbial*

A sentence element is any word or group of words in Swedish which can be moved to the beginning of a sentence (main clause statement):

Ikväll har vi inte köpt tidningen.
Tonight we haven't bought the paper.

Tidningen har vi inte köpt ikväll.
Literally: The paper we haven't bought today.

12.2 Sentence types

Most sentences possess both a subject (see 12.6.1) and a finite verb (see 12.6.2).

1 In describing clauses we often use the terms FV1-clause, FV2-clause.

In FV1-clauses the finite verb comes first in the sentence.
In FV2-clauses the finite verb comes second, after some other element.

2 The five sentence types in Swedish are shown in the table below.

S = subject
straight (word order) = subject – finite verb
inverted (word order) = finite verb – subject

Position:1	2	3	4–7	Word order
Statement				
	Subject	*Finite verb*	*etc.*	
	Han	**kommer**	**hem idag.**	*FV-2, straight*
Non-subject	*Finite verb*	*Subject*	*etc.*	
Idag	**kommer**	**han**	**hem.**	*FV-2, inverted*
Yes/no questions				
	Finite verb	*Subject*	*etc.*	
	Kommer	**han**	**hem idag?**	*FV-1, inverted*
	Ska	**han**	**inte komma hem idag?**	*FV-1, inverted*
V-question				
V-word	*Finite verb*	*Subject*	*etc.*	
Varför	**kommer**	**han**	**hem idag?**	*FV-2, inverted*
Vem	**kommer**	–	**hem idag?**	*FV-2, straight*
S				
Vad	**händer**	–	**därborta?**	*FV-2, straight*
S				
Command				
	Finite verb	*Subject*	*etc.*	
	Kom	–	**hem nu!**	*FV-1, no subject*
Wish				
	Finite verb	*Subject*	*etc.*	
	Må	**det**	**gå dig väl!**	*FV-1, inverted*
	(Subjunctive)			
	Leve	**brudparet!** –		*FV-1, inverted*
Subject	*Finite verb*	–	*etc.*	
Det	**vore**	–	**roligt att träffas!**	*FV-2, straight*

Translations: He's coming home today. Today he's coming home. Is he coming home today? Won't he come home today? Why is he coming home today? Who is coming home today? What's happening over there? Come home now! May it go well for you! Long live the bride and groom! It would be fun to meet up.

Notes:

1 *V-questions* begin with an interrogative pronoun or **v**-word (see 5.11).

2 *Yes/no questions* are so called because the answer to them is often 'yes' or 'no'.

3 Notice the difference between **v**-questions (FV2) and yes/no questions (FV1).

12.3 Main clause structure

Many main clause sentences possess other elements not mentioned in 12.2 above. These are included in the scheme below, which may be used to analyse most main clause sentences in Swedish.

1 Topic	2 Finite verb	3 Subject	4 Clausal adverbial	5 Non-finite verb	6 Object/ Complement	7 Other adverbial
Statement						
Han (S)	**kommer**	–	–	–	–	**hem idag.**
Imorse	**hade**	**han**	**ännu inte**	**packat**	**väskan.**	
Väskan	**hade**	**han**	**ännu inte**	**packat**	–	**i morse.**
Sedan	**blev**	**de**	**tyvärr**	–	**arga.**	
Yes/no question						
	Kommer	**de**	**aldrig**	–	–	**till Malmö?**
	Brukar	**de**	**aldrig**	**komma**	–	**till Malmö?**
V-question						
Vem (S)	**kommer**	–	–	–	–	**hit ikväll?**
Vem (O)	**gav**	**du**	–	–	**pengarna till?**	
När	**tänker**	**de**	–	**åka**	–	**till Norge?**
Command						
	Ring	–	**alltid**	–	–	**före tolv!**
Wish						
	Må	**du**	**aldrig**	**få ångra**	**dig!**	
	Leve	**kungen!**				
Det (S)	**vore**	–	**inte**	–	**så dumt!**	

Key: (S) = subject, (O) = object

Translations: He's coming home today. This morning he still hadn't packed the case. (*Lit.:* The case he still hadn't packed this morning.) Then, alas, they got angry. Do they never come to Malmö? Don't they ever come to Malmö? Who's coming here tonight? Who did you give the money to? When are they thinking of going to Norway? Always ring before twelve! May you never regret it! Long live the king! That wouldn't be such a bad idea!

Notes:

1   Main clause sentences always have a finite verb and usually a subject.
2   All positions except those occupied by the finite verb may be left vacant.
3   The subject usually occupies positions 1 or 3 (see 12.6.1).
4   The topic position is always occupied in statements and **v**-questions, but is vacant in yes/no questions.
5   Only one sentence element at a time may occupy the topic position (see 12.7.1).
6   There may be more than one finite verb, clausal adverbial, non-finite verb, object, complement or several other adverbials.
7   **V**-words may be subject or object in **v**-questions.

12.4 Link position

The link position (L) is an additional position necessary before the topic in order to accommodate conjunctions:

	L	T	FV	S	CA	NFV	O/C	OA
Han kommer,	**men**	**han**	**tänker**	–		**inte**	**stanna** –	**länge.**
Kommer du,	**eller**	–	**stannar**	**du**	–		– –	**hemma?**

Translations: He is coming but he's not thinking of staying long. Are you coming or are you staying at home?

12.5 Extra positions

The extra positions (X^1, X^2) are additional positions necessary both before the topic position and after the OA position to accommodate elements of various kinds outside the clause. These elements often duplicate elements within the clause proper.

	X^1	T	FV	S	CA	NFV	O/C	OA	X^2
1	**Olle,**	**han**	**är**	–	**ju**	–	**sjuk**	**idag,**	**han.**
2	**Paris,**	**det**	**är**	–	**väl**	–	**en vacker stad.**		
3		**Inte**	**gör**	**vi**	–	–	**det,**	–	**inte!**
4	**I Lund,**	**där**	**vill**	**jag**	–	**bo.**			
5	**När vi kom fram,**	**så**	**kokade**	**vi**	–	–	**kaffe.**		
6		**Det**	**är**	–	**inte**	–	**sant**	–	**att tiden läker alla sår.**

See also 12.6.1, 12.7.7.

	X^1	T	FV	S	CA	NFV	O/C	OA	X^2
7		**Det**	**är**	–	–	–	**roligt**	–	**att spela tennis.**

Translations: 1 Olle, he's ill today of course, he is. 2 (Now) Paris, that's a beautiful city. 3 We're not doing that, we're not. 4 In Lund, that's where I want to live. 5 When we got there we made coffee. 6 It isn't true that time heals all wounds. 7 It is fun to play tennis.

If there is also a link position, the order is:

L	X¹	T etc.
men	**Olle,**	**han är rolig** . . .
but	Olle,	he's funny

12.6 Main clause positions (sentence elements)

12.6.1 Subject and formal subject

The subject (S) may be:

- a noun phrase: **Snön ligger djupt.** The snow lies deep.
  Annika åker skidor. Annika goes skiing.
- a pronoun: **Han äter middag.** He is eating dinner.
- an adjective: **Rött är väl vackert.** Red is beautiful, isn't it?
- a verb: **Att ljuga är fult.** Lying is bad.
- a subordinate clause: **Att vi förlorade** That we lost the match
  matchen är synd is a pity.

The formal subject (FS) **det** must be inserted when there is a postponed or real subject (RS):

> **Det** (FS) **sitter en hund** (S) **i vardagsrummet.**
> There's a dog sitting in the living room.
> (Cf. **En hund sitter i vardagsrummet.**)

12.6.2 Finite verb

The finite verb (FV) is the verb which carries the tense, i.e. which indicates present or past time. The finite forms are, therefore, the present, past, imperative and subjunctive forms.

Han springer fort.	He is *running* fast.
Han sprang fort.	He *ran* fast.
Spring fortare!	*Run* faster!

In two-verb constructions the finite verb is often a modal or modal equivalent verb:

De kan springa fort.	They *can* run fast.

12.6.3 Non-finite verb

The non-finite verb (NFV) usually occurs together with a finite verb (12.6.2). Non-finite forms include the infinitive, supine, present participle and past participle.

De kan _springa_ fort.	They can run fast.
Vi har _sprungit_ hela vägen.	We have run the whole way.
De kom _springande_ nerför gatan.	They came running down the street.
Hunden är _bortsprungen_ nu.	The dog has run off now.

12.6.4 Clausal adverbial

1 The clausal adverbial (CA) modifies the sense of the clause as a whole. It is often a simple adverb:

FV	CA	etc.	
Vi åker	_inte_	till Sverige på sommaren.	= not
	alltid		= always
	aldrig		= never
	ofta		= often
	sällan		= seldom
	faktiskt		= actually
	_ju_		= of course

Cf. Word order in the English main clause:

	CA	FV	
We	_never_	go	to Sweden in the summer.

2 Clausal adverbials are also called 'mobile qualifiers' as they adopt different positions in the main clause compared with the subordinate clause (see 12.3, 12.6.9, 12.7.5, 12.8.2, 12.8.3(2)).

3 Notice the relative order when there are several clausal adverbials:

(a) Short modal adverbs:	**ju, nog, väl, då**
(b) Short pronominal and conjunctional adverbs:	**alltså, därför, ändå**
(c) Longer modal adverbs:	**verkligen, egentligen, faktiskt**
(d) Negations:	**inte, aldrig**

De har _ju_ (1) _därför_ (2) _faktiskt_ (3) _aldrig_ (4) rest utomlands.
They have, you understand, therefore actually never been abroad.

12.6.5 Other adverbials

Other adverbials (OA) comprise expressions of manner, place, time, cause, condition, etc. They are sometimes called *MPT-adverbials* for this reason, and often consist of a preposition + noun construction or of a subordinate clause:

Vi kommer *med tåg.* OA-manner	We're coming by train.
Vi kommer *till Stockholm.* OA-place	We're coming to Stockholm.
Vi kommer *på torsdag.* OA-time	We're coming on Thursday.
Vi kommer *om vi har tid.* OA-condition	We'll come if we have time.
Vi kommer *när vi är lediga.* OA-time	We'll come when we are free.

Notice that the relative order of OAs is usually (but not always):

Vi kommer *med tåg* (Manner) *till Stockholm* (Place) *på torsdag* (Time) *om vi har tid* (Condition).
We're coming by train to Stockholm on Thursday if we have time.

If the adverbial of manner is long, however, the order may be PTM:

Han reser till Frankrike på sommaren med egen bil.
He travels by car to France in the summer.

Some simple adverbs are also OAs:

Vi kom dit/hem/ut/bort/ner.
We got there/home/out/down.

OAs usually come at the end of sentences but often begin main clauses. See 12.7.1.

12.6.6 Objects and complements

Transitive verbs (7.5.14) take a direct object:		**Nils äter kakan.**
Intransitive verbs (7.5.14) take no object:		**Nils sitter i soffan.**

The direct object (DO) – which goes in the object (O) position – may comprise:

Main clause positions (sentence elements)

a noun phrase:	**Någon stal** *hans bil.*	Someone stole his car.
a pronoun:	**Anna kysste** *honom.*	Anna kissed him.
a subordinate clause:	**Jag vet** *att han är där.*	I know that he is there.

Ditransitive verbs possess both a direct and an indirect object (see 7.5.14).

The indirect object (IO) is usually a person for whose sake an action is undertaken:

Jag gav *studenten min bok.*	**Jag gav** *min bok till studenten.*
IO DO	DO IO
I gave the student my book.	I gave my book to the student.

Notice that the order of the objects is usually as in English, i.e.:

- a prepositionless object precedes an object with a preposition:

Han lånade	*boken*	*till Nils.*
	– prep	+ prep
He lent	the book	to Nils.

- if neither object has a preposition the indirect object precedes the direct object:

Han lånade	*Nils*	*boken.*
	IO	DO
He lent	Nils	the book.

The predicative complement (C) occupies the same position as the object (O), following the object if there is one. It is found in sentences with *copular* verbs such as: **vara, bli, heta, kallas, verka, tyckas, se . . . ut, utse . . . till, göra . . . till.** The complement agrees with the subject or object.

Subject complements

| **Olle och Mari är** *studenter.* | Olle and Mari are students. |
| **De blir säkert** *nervösa.* | They will surely get nervous. |

Object complements

| **Det gjorde honom** *besviken.* | They made him disappointed. |
| **De kallade Sture för** *Stumpen.* | They called Sture 'Stumpen'. |

12.6.7 Verb particle

See compound verbs, 7.5.18. The verb particle (Part) occupies a position between the non-finite verb and the object/complement:

1	2	3	4	5	5a	6	7
T	FV	S	CA	NFV	Part	O/C	OA
Jag	**tycker**	–	**inte**	–	**om**	**honom.**	
	Har	**du**	**aldrig**	**tyckt**	**om**	**henne?**	
Du	**kommer**	–	**nog**	**att tycka**	**om**	**henne.**	

Translations: I don't like him. Have you never liked her? You will probably like her.

12.6.8 Passive agent

See passive, 7.5.17, 12.7.6. The passive agent (Agent) occupies a position between the object/complement and the other adverbial:

1	2	3	4	5	6	6a	7
T	FV	S	CA	NFV	O/C	Agent	OA
Han	**blev**	–	**inte**	**omkörd**	–	*av bussen.*	
Han	**beviljades**	–	–		**avsked**	*av styrelsen*	**igår.**

Translations: He was not overtaken by the bus. He was allowed to resign by the board yesterday.

12.6.9 Main clause structure – extended positional scheme with examples

	1 T	2 FV	3 (S)	4 CA	5 NFV	5a Part	6 O/C	6a	7 Agent	L OA	X¹ X²
1	Han	hade	–	inte	packat	–	väskan		–	imorse.	
2	Imorse	hade	han	inte	packat	–	väskan.				
3	Vi	ger	–	–	–	–	Olle	gåvan	–	ikväll.	
4	Sedan	blev	de	tyvärr	–		arga.				
5	Det	har	–	redan	kommit	–	två poliser.				
6	och det	är	–	ju	–	–	roligt	–	–		att spela tennis.
7	Sten	brukade	–		kyssa	–	oss,	–	–		Maja och mig.
8	men Nils, han	är	–	inte	–	–	dum,	–	–		han.
9	De	ringde	–	–	–	upp	oss	–	–	hemma.	
10	Vi	blev	–	–	–	upp-ringda	–	–	av Olssons	hemma.	
11	Far	dödades	–	–	–	–	–	–	–	under kriget.	
12	De	gifte	sig	aldrig.							
13	Vi	känner	honom	inte.							

Translations: 1 He hadn't packed the case this morning. 2 This morning he hadn't packed the case. 3 We will give Olle the gift tonight. 4 Then they unfortunately got angry. 5 Two policemen have already arrived. 6 and it is of course fun to play tennis. 7 Sten used to kiss us, Maja and me. 8 but Nils, he's not stupid, he isn't. 9 They rang us up at home. 10 We were rung up by the Olssons at home. 11 Father was killed during the war. 12 They never married. 13 We don't know him.

Key to table:

		For details see section:
L(ink) = conjunction		12.4
X¹ = extra position	duplicate elements in the sentence	12.5
T(opic)	any sentence element	12.7.1
F(inite) V(erb)	verb carrying the tense	12.6.2
S(ubject)	includes reflexive pronoun, unstressed object	12.6.1
C(lausal) A(dverbial)		12.6.4
N(on-) F(inite) V(erb)	infinitive, supine or participle	12.6.3
(Verb) Part(icle)	only with separable compound verbs	12.6.7
O(bject)/C(omplement)	includes real subject	12.6.6
Agent	only with passive verbs	12.6.8
O(ther) A(dverbials)	manner, place, time, etc.	12.6.5
X² – extra position	duplicates elements in the sentence, subject and object clauses and non-finite clauses	12.5
Sentences 2, 4		12.7.1
Sentence 3		12.6.6
Sentences 5, 6		12.7.7
Sentences 7, 8		12.5
Sentence 9		12.6.7
Sentence 10		12.6.8
Sentences 12, 13		12.7.4

12.7 **Moving elements within the main clause**

12.7.1 *Topicalization*

1 The subject most frequently occupies the topic position, but it may be replaced by moving to the front almost any other sentence element. When the subject is not the topic it follows the finite verb.

	T	FV	S	CA	NFV	O	OA
Base sentence:							
	Han	**tänker**	–	inte	sälja	bilen	i år.
New topic 1 (OA to topic):							
	I år	**tänker**	han	inte	sälja	bilen.	–
New topic 2 (O to topic):							
	Bilen	**tänker**	han	inte	sälja	–	i år.
	Det	**tänker**	vi	inte	göra.		
New topic 3 (CA to topic):							
	Inte	**tänker**	han	–	sälja	bilen	i år.
New topic 4 (Verb phrase to topic):							
	Sälja bilen	**tänker**	han	inte	(göra) –		i år.
Note other possible topics:							
Direct speech to topic:							
	Tusan!	**sa**	han.				
Complement to topic:							
	Vacker	**var**	han	inte.			

Translations: He's not thinking of selling the car this year. This year he's not thinking of selling the car. (*Lit.*: The car he is not thinking of selling this year.) We're not thinking of doing that. (Surely) he's not thinking of selling the car this year! Selling the car (is something) he's not thinking of doing this year. 'Blast!' he said. Beautiful he was not.

Topicalization of other adverbials (especially time, place) is by far the most frequent type:

Vi åkte till Lund i våras.   →   *I våras* **åkte vi till Lund.**

→   *Till Lund* **åkte vi i våras.**

The OA, topicalized or not, often consists of a subordinate clause:

Vi åkte till Lund när   →   **När vi kom hem åkte**
vi kom hem.   **vi till Lund.**

Translations: We went to Lund last spring. Last spring we went to Lund. To Lund we went last spring. We went to Lund when we got home. When we got home we went to Lund.

2 Natural topics

Most natural topics are unstressed and represent familiar information or are used to link sentences together:

Vi behövde en semester, så *i somras* reste vi till Värmland.
***Där* träffade vi några gamla vänner. *De* har en stor villa.**
***Den* har tio rum. *Vi* bodde där en hel vecka. *Sedan* måste vi**
tyvärr resa hem igen.

Translations: We needed a holiday, so last summer we went to Värmland. There we met some old friends. They have a big house. It has ten rooms. We lived there for a whole week. Then alas we had to come home again.

3 Emphatic topics

These are rarer and often represent new information. The following emphatic topics are either stylistically marked or used for contrast:

***Förskräckligt* är det. *En tidning* köpte vi också. *Det* kan jag**
aldrig tro på. *I fjol* dog han (inte i år). *Springa efter flickor* kan
han, men *studera* vill han inte.

Translations: (*Lit*.: Terrible it is.) (*Lit*.: A newspaper we bought too.) That I can never believe. Last year he died (not this year). (*Lit*.: Run after girls he can, but study he will not.)

| 12.7.2 | *Weight principle*

The weight principle is revealed in different structures in 12.7.3–12.7.7 below. It can be formulated as follows: unstressed familiar information (a short element) tends to be placed to the left in the sentence, while heavy new information (a long element) tends to be placed to the right in the sentence. Thus the balance in most sentences is 'right-heavy'.

193

1 The principle means that elements losing their stress may move leftwards (+/– indicates +stress/ –stress):

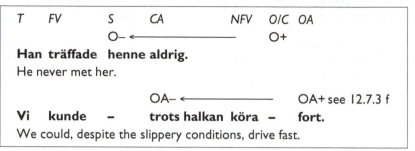

T	FV	S	CA		NFV	O/C	OA
		O– ⟵ ———————				O+	

Han träffade henne aldrig.
He never met her.

			OA– ⟵ ———————				OA+ see 12.7.3 f

Vi   kunde   –   trots halkan köra   –   fort.
We could, despite the slippery conditions, drive fast.

2 Occasionally, as in the case of **inte**, this leftward movement is not accommodated within the positional scheme:

T	FV		S	CA	NFV	O/C	OA
		⟵ ———————		inte	see 12.7.5		

Dricker inte   Olle   –   –   vin?
Doesn't Olle drink wine?

3 Some elements that are stressed, such as subjects introducing new information, may be postponed (moved rightwards):

T	FV	S	CA	NFV	O/C	OA	X^2
S(NP)+ ——————————⟶					S(NP)+		

Det   har   –   inte kommit   några brev idag.
No letters have come today.

S(IP/subcl)+ ——————————————⟶						S(IP/subcl)+	

Det   är   –   –   –   tråkigt   –   att få vänta
**   på brev.**

It's annoying having to wait for letters.

Notes:

    (NP = indefinite noun phrase, IP = infinitive phrase, subcl = subordinate clause) see 12.7.7.

    Det (place holder subject) replaces the subject in this case.

4 In passive transformation both leftward and rightward movements occur simultaneously:

T	FV	S	CA	NFV	O/C	Agent	OA
A–					B+		
En flicka **körde**		–	–	–	*lastbilen.*		
A girl drove the truck.							

↙ ↘

T	FV	S	CA	NFV	O/C	Agent	OA
B–						(A+)	see 12.7.6
Lastbilen **kördes**		–	–	–	–	*av en flicka.*	
The truck was driven by a girl.							

12.7.3 Adverbial shift

The OA may occupy the OA or T positions, but may also be moved to the CA position in order to leave an element in the final stressed position:

Han utnämndes till generalsekreterare i FN *1953* (OA).
He was appointed Secretary General of the United Nations in 1953.

Han utnämndes *1953* (OA) **till generalsekreterare i FN.**
He was in 1953 appointed Secretary General of the United Nations.

Moving the OA leftwards may make the expression more formal:

Han har stannat hemma *under de senaste dagarna* (OA).
He has stayed home over the past few days.

Han har *under de senaste dagarna* (OA) **stannat hemma.**
He has over the past few days stayed home.

Jag brukar tillbringa semestern i Spanien *varje år* (OA).
I usually spend the holidays in Spain every year.

Jag brukar *varje år* (OA) **tillbringa semestern i Spanien.**
I usually every year spend the holidays in Spain.

12.7.4 Unstressed objects

Unstressed object pronouns and reflexive pronouns often move leftwards into the subject position. This occurs only with a simple verb (present, past).

T	FV	S O −stress	CA	NFV	O/C O +stress	OA
Jag	känner	–	inte	–	honom.	
Jag	känner	honom	inte.			
Han	fick	–	inte	–	det.	
Han	fick	det	inte.			
Olle	tvättar	sig	inte.			
(cf. Olle	har	–	inte	tvättat	sig	idag.)

Translations: I don't know *him*. I don't know him. He didn't get that. He didn't get it. Olle doesn't wash. Olle hasn't washed today.

12.7.5 Position of inte

The position of **inte** (and **icke, ej, aldrig** as well as other clausal adverbials) varies. In the main clause **inte** comes immediately *after* the finite verb or subject (see 12.3, 12.6.4):

Peter kommer inte idag.   Peter isn't coming today.

Idag kommer Peter inte.   Today Peter isn't coming.

Idag har Peter inte kommit.   Today Peter hasn't come.

In the subordinate clause **inte** comes immediately *before* the finite verb (see 12.8.2):

Olle sa, att Peter inte kommer idag.
          S   I   V   SIV = subject-**inte**-verb
Olle said that Peter isn't coming today.

One exception to this word order in the main clause has been shown in 12.7.4, where the unstressed object intrudes between the verb and **inte**. Another exception is found in cases like the following:

Idag kommer inte 'Peter (men Olle kommer).
cf. **Idag kommer Peter 'inte (men han kommer imorgon).**

Here **inte** precedes the subject in a main clause so that **Peter** remains in the stress position at the end of the sentence.

Other cases in which **inte** is moved from its usual position result from a
desire to restrict its effect from negating the entire clause to negating only
a word or group of words:

Alla pojkar ljuger inte.	=	either:	Some boys do not lie.
		or:	No boys lie.
Inte alla pojkar ljuger.	=		Not all boys lie(, but some do).

12.7.6 Passive transformation

By transforming the active verb into a passive form, elements may be
moved radically within the clause:

Active verb	*Eleverna* (S) **tyckte mycket om** *henne* (O).
	The pupils liked her a lot.
Passive verb	*Hon* (S) **var mycket omtyckt** *av eleverna* (Agent) **(men inte av kollegorna).**
	She was much liked by the pupils (but not by her colleagues).

Passive transformation can be used in either main or subordinate clauses
(cf. topicalization, 12.7.1). For the position of elements in the passive
sentence, see 12.6.9, examples 10, 11.

12.7.7 Existential sentence

If we do not wish to introduce a subject containing new, heavy information
too soon, we can postpone the subject (i.e. move it rightwards in the
sentence), but must then fill the topic position in a statement with a formal
subject (place holder subject):

***En polis* sitter i köket. →**	***Det***	**sitter**	***en polis* i köket.**
Subject	Formal subject		Real subject
A policeman is sitting in the kitchen.	There's a policeman sitting in the kitchen.		
***Att sluta röka* är svårt. →**	***Det är svårt***		***att sluta röka.***
Subject	FS		RS
Stopping smoking is difficult.	It's difficult to stop smoking.		

Type 1: When the real subject is an indefinite noun phrase (like **en polis**)
then it occupies the O/C position.

T	FV	S	CA	NFV	O/C	OA	X^2
Det	**finns**	–	–	–	***ingen ketchup***	**hemma.**	
Det	**sitter**	–	**ofta**	–	***en polis***	**i köket.**	
	Sitter	**det**	**ofta**	–	***en polis***	**i köket?**	

Translations: There's no ketchup in the house. There's often a policeman sitting in the kitchen. Is there often a policeman sitting in the kitchen?

The verb in Swedish existential sentences is always intransitive, and usually
expresses:

Existence:	**finnas**
Non-existence:	**fattas, saknas**
Location:	**vara, sitta, stå, ligga**
Motion:	**komma, gå**

In English the only corresponding constructions are: 'there is/are -ing'.

Type 2: When the real subject is an infinitive phrase (like **att sluta röka**)
then it occupies the X^2 position (see 12.5, 12.6.1):

T	FV	S	CA	NFV	O/C	OA	X^2
Det	**är**	–	–	–	**troligt**	–	***att han vinner.***
Det	**har**	–	**alltid**	**varit**	**en gåta för mig**	–	***varför han fick***
							nobelpriset.

Translations: It is probable that he will win. It's always been a mystery to me why he
got the Nobel Prize.

Note that in this case **det** = 'it'.

12.7.8 Cleft sentence

In order to emphasize an element together with the action of the verb, that element (W) may be extracted from the sentence and inserted into the construction:

Det är/var (W) som ...

The remainder of the original sentence is downgraded and relegated to the **som**-clause added onto the end:

Cf. **Anders skickade mig en bok förra veckan.**
Anders sent me a book last week.

→   **Det var *en bok* (W) som Anders skickade mig förra veckan (inte en CD-skiva)**

→   **Det var *Anders* (W) som skickade mig en bok förra veckan (inte Göran)**

→   **Det var *förra veckan* (W) som Anders skickade mig en bok (inte den här veckan)**

Translations: It was a book that Anders ... It was Anders who ... It was last week that ...

The cleft sentence is also very common in questions:

Var det *oppositionsledaren* (W) som kritiserade regeringen?
Was it the Leader of the Opposition who criticized the government?
(cf. **Kritiserade oppositionsledaren regeringen?**)

Är det *jag* (W) som måste bestämma?
Is it me who must decide?

Är det *öl* (W) som han dricker?
Is it beer he's drinking?

12.8 Subordinate clauses

12.8.1 Subordinate clause as an element in the main clause sentence

1 Subordinate clauses usually constitute the subject, object or other adverbial in a main clause sentence. As such they may occupy several different positions. In looking at the main clause in this way we can talk of first stage analysis (cf. 12.8.2):

T	FV	S	CA	NFV	O/C	OA	X^2
Subject clause:							
Att du är frisk	**gläder**	–	–	–	**mig**.		
Det	**gläder**	–	–	–	**mig**	–	*att du är frisk.*
Object clause:							
Han	**sa**	–	inte	–	–	igår	*att han skulle bort.*
Att han skulle bort	**sa**	han	inte	–	–	igår.	
Adverbial clause:							
Vi	**åker**	–	–	–	–	*när han kommer.*	
När han kommer	**åker**	vi.					

Translations: That you are better pleases me. It pleases me that you are better. He didn't say yesterday that he was going away. (*Lit.:* That he was going away he didn't say yesterday.) We'll leave when he comes. When he comes we'll leave.

Adverbial clauses also begin with: **därför att, eftersom, fast(än), innan, medan, om, sedan, trots att.**

Note that:

(a) Subject and object clauses occupy the T or X^2 positions.
(b) Most adverbial clauses (time, condition, cause) occupy the T, CA or OA positions.
(c) Some adverbial clauses (result) may only occupy the OA position:

T	FV	S	CA	NFV	O/C	OA
Man	**måste**	–	–	**stödja**	**honom**	*för att han inte ska falla.*
Jag	**var**	–	–	–	**så arg**	*att jag genast gick därifrån.*

Translations: One has to support him so that he doesn't fall. I was so angry that I left immediately.

2 A relative clause usually functions as an attribute to a noun (subject, object) and begins with the indeclinable **som** (**där**, **dit**):

Han tittade på flickorna (O) *som satt på bänken.*
He looked at the girls who were sitting on the bench.

Filmen (S) *som vi gick på* **var fantastisk.**
The film that we went to was fantastic.

3 An independent clause is a subordinate clause which stands alone as a sentence and does not form part of a larger main clause sentence. It is usually an exclamation or wish:

Conj.	S	CA	FV	NFV	O/C	OA
Om	**du**	**bara**	**visste**	–	**allt!**	
Att	**ni**	**inte**	**blir**	–	**trötta!**	

Translations: If you only knew everything! (*Lit.:* That you don't get tired!)

| **12.8.2** | **Subordinate clause structure** |

Subordinate clauses (which may be elements in main clause sentences) also possess an internal structure of their own. In looking at this we may talk of second stage analysis (cf. 12.8.1):

Matrix	I Conj.	2 S	3 CA	4 FV	5 NFV	6 O/C	7 OA
Vi åker	**när**	han	kommer.				
Vi frågade	**om**	de	inte	hade	packat	väskan.	
	Eftersom	de	inte	(hade)	sagt	ett ord,	–
visste vi inget.							
Vi tyckte,	**(att)**	det	inte	var	–	roligt	längre.
Om vi är							
tysta,	**och om**	vi	inte	busar,	–	–	–
får vi se på TV.							

Translations: We'll leave when he arrives. We asked whether they hadn't packed the case. As they hadn't said a word we knew nothing. We thought (that) it wasn't funny any longer. If we are quiet and if we're not naughty, we can watch TV.

Notice the following characteristics of the subordinate clause:

1 There is *no* topic in the subordinate clause; the order is always: conjunction – subject – CA – finite verb, i.e.

- the clause always begins with a subordinating conjunction or other subordinator (see 11.2 f).
- the clausal adverbial comes before the finite verb. (Remember S-I-V: Subject – **Inte** –Verb, 12.7.5)
- the word order is straight (S-FV).

2 The subject position is always occupied.

3 The conjunction **att** may sometimes be omitted.

4 The auxiliary **har/hade** may be omitted when there is a supine (in the NFV position). This omission of **har** is common in written Swedish, unusual in normal spoken Swedish.

5 Notice also that the adverbial splits the infinitive in Swedish:

Fredrik lovade (att) *inte* (CA) säga något.
Fredrik promised not to say anything.

Jag hoppas (att) *snart* (CA) få träffa dig igen.
I hope to meet you again soon.

Jag hoppas att *i min nuvarande ställning* (OA) fortsätta att tjäna mitt land.
I hope in my present position to continue to serve my country.

| 12.8.3 | *Three types of subordinate clause with main clause structure* |

These are all exceptions, in different ways, to 12.8.2 above, in that the subordinate clause forms part of a main clause sentence (cf. 12.8.1) but has a word order that is similar to that of the main clause (see 12.3).

1 Att-clauses with a 'topic':

When a non-subject comes immediately after the conjunction **att**, the finite verb and subject are inverted:

	Conj.	'Topic'	FV	S
Fredrik sa,	**att**	**igår**	**tänkte**	**han åka till stan.**

Fredrik said that yesterday he was thinking of going to town.

2 Att-clauses with FV-CA order:

In some cases the clausal adverbial adopts the same position as in the main clause, i.e. *after* the finite verb, rather than its usual subordinate clause position *before* the finite verb:

	Conj.	S	FV	CA
Fredrik sa,	**att**	**han**	**tänkte**	**inte åka idag.**

Fredrik said that he was not thinking of leaving today.

This is only found in spoken Swedish.

Write:	Conj.	S	CA	FV
Fredrik sa,	**att**	**han**	**inte**	**tänkte åka idag.**

An explanation for this order is that the **att**-clause is regarded as a statement in direct speech, i.e. as a main clause. Cf.:

Fredrik sa: 'Jag tänker inte åka idag'.
Fredrik said 'I am not thinking of leaving today'.

The conjunction **att** then functions almost as a colon.

3 Conditional clauses with yes/no question order:

Conditional clauses are usually introduced by **om** or **ifall**:

Om du inte skriver till mor, blir hon ledsen.
If you don't write to Mum, she will be upset.

But conditional clauses are also found which possess no subordinating conjunction, and rely on inverted word order (FV-S) to indicate condition:

Skriver du inte till mor, blir hon ledsen.
cf. **Skriver du inte till mor?** (Yes/no question)

Clauses of this type also occur in English:

Had I known when you were arriving, I would have waited.
Hade jag vetat när du skulle komma, skulle jag ha väntat.

Were you to agree to this, it would be disastrous.
Skulle du gå med på detta, vore det katastrofalt.

12.9 Differences between Swedish and English word order

12.9.1 Major word order and sentence structure problems – summary

A number of aspects of word order are similar in Swedish and English. This summary concentrates only on the differences.

Key: S = subject FV = finite verb CA = clausal adverbial
      T = sentence element (non-subject) which may come first in the sentence
      W = word(s) moved for emphasis or presented as a new subject

1 Main clause – inversion (12.2 ff, 12.6.9, 12.7.1)

Swedish: English:
S – FV – T   S – FV – T
Vi åker hem nu.   We're going home now.

In Swedish non-subjects often come first in the main clause, and this causes inversion of subject and finite verb.

T – FV – S   T – S – FV
Nu åker vi hem.   Now we're going home.

In English the order is usually subject – verb. (cf. however: Up went the lift.)

2 Main clause – adverb(ial)s (i.e. **inte, aldrig**) (12.2–12.5, 12.6.4, 12.7.5)

S – FV – CA	S – CA – FV
De leker aldrig.	They never play.

In main clauses in Swedish the clausal adverbial (adverb) usually comes immediately *after* the finite verb. In English it usually comes immediately *before* the finite verb.

3 Subordinate clause – adverb(ial)s (i.e. **inte, aldrig**) (12.7.5, 12.8.2)

S – CA – FV	S – FV – CA
De sade, att de inte hade skrivit.	They said that they had not written.
De vet att jag aldrig dricker.	They know I never drink.

In subordinate clauses in Swedish the clausal adverbial (adverb) always comes immediately *before* the finite verb.

Remember: S-I-V : Subject – **Inte** – Verb. In English the position varies.

4 Adverbs split the infinitive (12.8.2)

	att – CA – NFV(inf)
Vi bad honom	**att genast sluta röka.**
	to – NFV(inf) – CA
We asked him	to stop smoking immediately.

5 Emphasizing part of a clause (12.7.8)

A word or words to be emphasized (W) may be extracted from a clause and placed in this special construction. The rest of the sentence is downgraded to a subordinate clause after **som**. W can represent most elements in a Swedish clause.

Base clause	**Anders skickade mig en bok förra veckan.**
	Anders sent me a book last week.
Det är/var (W) som . . .	**Det var *en bok* som Anders skickade mig förra veckan.**
Vem/Vad är det som . . .?	**Vem var det som skickade mig en bok . . .?**
	Vad var det som Anders skickade mig . . .?

205

Var det (W) som . . .?

**Var det *en bok* som Anders
skickade mig . . .?
Var det *Anders* som skickade mig
en bok . . .?
Var det *förra veckan* som Anders
skickade mig en bok?**

6 Presenting a new subject (12.7.7)

S – FV	S – FV
En polis sitter i köket.	A policeman is sitting in the kitchen.

Det – FV – S	There is – S – FV-ing
Det sitter en polis i köket.	There is a policeman sitting in the kitchen.

Questions:

FV – **det** – S	Is there – S – V-ing?
Sitter det ofta en polis i köket?	Is there often a policeman sitting . . .?

7 Objects, etc., with and without stress (12.7.4)

S – FV – CA – O	S – FV – CA – O
Jag känner inte *honom*.	I don't know *him*.

S – V – O – CA
Jag känner honom inte.

When objects lose their stress in Swedish they move left in the sentence.
In English voice stress is used.

8 Verb particles (12.6.7)

S – FV – Part – O	S – FV – O – Part
Jag ringde upp honom igår.	I rang him up yesterday.
Vi kastade bort dem.	We threw them away.

In Swedish the particle precedes the object pronoun. In English the particle
always follows the object pronoun.

Chapter 13

Word formation

The lexicon of Swedish is constantly being altered by four main processes:

1 Borrowing: French 'pièce'   → Swedish **pjäs**   play
2 Compounding: **ett hus + ett tak**   → **ett hustak**   house roof
3 Affixation: *o-* + **lycklig**   → **olycklig**   unhappy
4 Abbreviation: **fotografi**   → **foto**   photo

Borrowing from other languages involves the eventual assimilation of a loanword into the Swedish system of orthography, pronunciation and inflexion.

13.1   Compounding

1 The first element of a compound may be a noun, adjective, verb, pronoun, numeral, adverb, preposition or word group, while the second element is usually a noun, adjective or verb:

Noun + noun:	**bilresa**	Verb + noun:	**åksjuka**
	car journey		travel-sickness
Noun + adjective:	**hjärtlös**	Verb + adjective:	**körklar**
	heartless		ready to drive
Noun + verb:	**soltorka**	Verb + verb:	**frystorka**
	sun dry		freeze dry

For separable and inseparable compound verbs (particle verbs) see 7.5.18.

2 Compound nouns may be formed by four main methods:

Notice that the second element in compounds determines the gender and inflexion of the compound.

(a) Noun + Noun

en bil + ett däck → **ett bildäck**
a car   a tyre   a car tyre

(b) Noun (minus -a/-e) + Noun

en flicka + en skola → **en flickskola**
a girl   a school   a girls' school

en pojke + ett namn → **ett pojknamn**
a boy   a name   a boy's name

en lärare + ett yrke → **(ett) läraryrke**
a teacher   a profession   teaching profession

(c) Noun + s + Noun

en parkering + ett hus → **ett parkeringshus**
a car park   a building   a multi-storey car park

(d) (Noun + old case ending in -u/-o/-e/-a) + Noun

en vecka + ett slut → **ett veckoslut**
a week   an end   a weekend

en vara + ett hus → **ett varuhus**
a product   a building   a department store

New compounds formed by this last method are very rare.

Whether or not -s- is used as a link between nouns depends to some extent on the form of the elements (first element = FE). Generally speaking the following have s-link:

• Nouns whose FE ends in -(n)ing, -ling, -an, -nad, -(i)tet, -(a)tion, -het:

vandringsled   long distance footpath

älsklingsrätt   favourite dish

självkostnadspris   cost price

stationsinspektor   station master

- Nouns whose FE is itself a compound:

  cf. **fot + boll**   →   **fotboll**
      fotboll + s + lag   →   **fotbollslag**
      football   team   football team

Others:

skolboksförlag	schoolbook publisher
ordbildningslära	word-formation theory
daghemsföreståndare	day-nursery supervisor
bilbärgningskår	car-breakdown service
järnvägsövergång	railway crossing

13.2   Affixation

Affixation is carried out by adding a *prefix* or *suffix* to a *stem*. Whilst prefixes do not alter the word class or inflexion of the stem, suffixes are often employed for this very purpose:

cf.	**o-**	+	**vän**	**→ ovän**
	negative prefix		noun stem	noun
	'un-'		friend	enemy

	vänlig	+	**-het**	**→ vänlighet**
	adjective stem		noun suffix	noun
	friendly			friendliness

	färg		**+ -a**	**→ färga**
	noun stem		verb suffix	verb
	colour			to colour

Generally speaking prefixes and suffixes are much vaguer and simpler in meaning than the stems they modify.

1 Prefixes: What follows is a list of some frequent examples only.

	Prefix	Meaning	Example	English
(a) Negative and pejorative	o-	not, opposite of, bad, wrongly	**olycklig**	unhappy
	in-/im-/il-	– " –	**intolerant**	intolerant
	miss-	– " –	**misslyckas**	fail
	van-	– " –	**vantrivas**	be ill at ease
(b) Attitude	sam-	together with	**samarbete**	cooperation
	ko-	– " –	**koordinera**	coordinate
	mot-	against	**motståndare**	opponent
(c) Location and direction	före-	before	**företrädare**	predecessor
	efter-	after	**efterskrift**	postscript
	ex-	from	**exportera**	export
	an-	towards	**ankomma**	arrive
	und-	away from	**undkomma**	escape
	re-	again	**reorganisera**	reorganize
	gen-	again	**gengångare**	ghost
(d) Conversion: + verb suffix →verb	an- + -a	(transitivizing)	**anropa**	challenge
	för- + -a	make into	**förnya**	renew
	be- + -a	– " –	**befria**	liberate

2 Suffixes: What follows is a list of some frequent examples only.

	Suffix		Example	English
(a) Nouns denoting people	-are		**läsare**	reader
	-ande		**studerande**	student
	-ende		**gående**	pedestrian
	-ant		**emigrant**	emigrant
	-ent		**konsument**	consumer
	-ör		**frisör**	hairdresser
	-ing		**värmlänning**	person from Värmland
	-ist		**cyklist**	cyclist
feminines	-inna		**värdinna**	hostess
	-(er)ska		**sjuksköterska**	nurse
	-essa		**prinsessa**	princess (female)
	-ös		**dansös**	dancer
	-ris		**servitris**	waitress
(b) Nouns denoting activity	-(n)ing		**skrivning**	examination
	-ande		**skrivande**	writing
	-an		**början**	beginning

			jämförelse	comparison
	-else		saknad	regret
	-nad		recension	review
	-sion		realisation	sale
	-tion			
(c) Nouns denoting	-het		brottslighet	crime
status	-lek		storlek	size
	-dom		sjukdom	illness
	-skap		vänskap	friendship
	-nad		tystnad	silence
	-ska		ondska	evil
	-an		önskan	wish
	-else		frestelse	temptation
(d) Conversion:	-bar	possible to	körbar	driveable
verb > adj.	-lig	possible to	rörlig	mobile
	-abel	possible to	diskutabel	debatable
	-aktig	tendency	slösaktig	wasteful
	-sam	tendency	arbetsam	industrious
	-ig	tendency	slarvig	careless
(e) Conversion:	-enlig	according to	lagenlig	according to the law
noun → adj.	-mässig	corresponding to	planmässig	according to plan
	-vänlig	'friendly'	miljövänlig	environ- mentally friendly
	-aktig	characteristic of	svinaktig	swinish
	-artad	– " –	granitartad	like granite
	-(i)sk	belonging to	brittisk	British
	-ant	– " –	elegant	elegant
	-ent	– " –	intelligent	intelligent
(f) Conversion:	-a		färga	colour
			cykla	cycle
noun, adj	-era		paketera,	package up
			adressera,	address
→ verb			decentralisera	decentralize
	-na	become + adj	svartna,	blacken
			mörkna	darken
	-ja	make + adj.	glädja	please
	(+ *mutation*)	(transitivizing)		

3 Productive and non-productive affixes:

Productive affixes are those still being used to form derivatives whose meaning can easily be predicted from the form:

-bar = possible to, therefore: **tänkbar** = possible to think, **användbar** = possible to use, etc.

Non-productive affixes are those no longer used to form derivatives:

-lek: **kärlek**, **storlek**, etc.

Non-productive affixes may have been borrowed with many loanwords but have never been used to form any indigenous derivatives, e.g.:

Latin **kon-**: **konflikt**, **konsonant.**

13.3 Abbreviation

1 Abbreviation involves the loss of a morpheme or part of a morpheme:

	Whole morpheme lost	Part morpheme lost
(a) Initial reduction	**(bi)cykel** bicycle	**(automo)bil** automobile, car
(b) Final reduction	**bio(graf)** cinema	**lok(omotiv)** locomotive
	livs(medelsaffär) grocery shop	**el(ektricitet)** electricity
	foto(grafi) photograph	**kolla(tionera)** check
(c) Medial reduction	**te(kopps)fat** saucer	**mo(torho)tell** motel

2 Reduction + **-is**, **-a(n)** in colloquial Swedish:

kond(itori) café	+ **is** → **kondis**	**mor** mother	+ **a** → **morsa**
dag(hem) day nursery	+ **is** → **dagis**	**syster** sister	+ **a** → **syrra**
grat(ulerar) congratulations	+ **is** → **grattis**	**Margareta**	+ **a** → **Maggan**
god(saker) sweets	+ **is** → **godis**	**Elisabeth**	+ **a** → **Bettan**

3 Hypocorism:

Pet names for boys are often formed by shortening the vowel and adding -e:

Karl → Kalle; Nils → Nisse; Jan → Janne; Lars → Lasse; Olof → Olle

4 Acronyms:

When the reduction leaves only an initial letter for each element an acronym results:

(a) Alphabetisms: **bh** (= **bysthållare**), brassiere; **TV**; **VM** (= **världsmästarskap**), world championship.
(b) Respelling of alphabetisms: **behå, teve**.
(c) Acronyms pronounced as words: **SAAB** [sɑ:b], **ASEA** [asɛ:a], **NATO** [nɑ:tɷ], **SAS** [sas].
(d) Hybrid forms: **p-plats** (**parkeringsplats**), car park; **T-bana** (**tunnelbana**), underground.

13.4 List of common abbreviations

These abbreviations are often found without full stops.

AB	Aktiebolag	Co. Ltd, PLC
ang.	angående	re
anm.	anmärkning	note
ansl.	anslutning	tel. extension
bil.	bilaga	enclosure
bl.a.	bland annat	inter alia
ca, c., c:a	cirka	approximately
do, d:o	dito	ditto
dvs, d.v.s.	det vill säga	i.e.
d.y.	den yngre	the younger
dyl.	dylikt	similar
dåv.	dåvarande	the then
d.ä.	den äldre	the elder
e.d., el.dyl.	eller dylikt	or similar
eg.	egentligen	really
e.Kr.	efter Kristus	A.D.
el, e., l.	eller	or

el	elektrisk	electrical
em, e.m.	eftermiddag	p.m.
enl.	enligt	according to
ev.	eventuellt	possibly
ex.	exempel	example
	exemplar	copy, copies
f.	förre	former
	följande	following
f.d.	före detta	ex-
f.Kr.	före Kristus	B.C.
fm, f.m.	förmiddag	a.m.
f.n.	för närvarande	at present
forts.	fortsättning	continued
fr.o.m.	från och med	with effect from
f.ö.	för övrigt	otherwise
följ.	följande	following
föreg.	föregående	previous
förf.	författare	author
förk.	förkortning	abbreviation
ggr	gånger	times
g.m.	gift med	married to
hr	herr	Mr
i allm.	i allmänhet	generally
inb.	inbunden	hard cover
inkl.	inklusive	including
inv.	invånare	inhabitant(s)
i st.f.	i stället för	instead of
jfr.	jämför	cf., compare
jvstn	järnvägsstation	railway station
kap.	kapitel	chapter
kl.	klockan	o'clock, at (a time)
	klass	class
kr.	kronor	kronor
l.	eller	or
m.a.o.	med andra ord	in other words
m.fl.	med flera	etc.
m.m.	med mera	etc.
motsv.	motsvarande	corresponding to
m.ö.h.	meter över havet	metres above sea level
möjl.	möjligen	possibly
NB	nedre botten	lower ground floor

nr	nummer	No., number	List of common abbreviations
nuv.	nuvarande	present	
o.	och	and	
o.a.	och annat	etc.	
Obs!	observera	NB, notice	
o.d., o.dyl.	och dylikt	and the like	
omkr.	omkring	approx.	
osv, o.s.v.	och så vidare	etc.	
p.g.a.	på grund av	because	
PM	promemoria	memorandum	
r.	rad	line	
red.	redaktör	editor	
s.	sida	page	
	sekund	second	
	substantiv	noun	
	subjekt	subject	
	söder	south	
	socialdemokrat	Social Democrat	
sa., s:a	summa	total	
s.a.s.	så att säga	so to speak	
sg.	singular(is)	singular	
s.o.h.	söndagar och helgdagar	Sundays and bank holidays	
s.k.	så kallad	so-called	
sms.	sammansättning	compound	
st.	styck(en)	number; each	
S:t, S:ta	sankt, sankta	(male) saint, (female) saint	
t.	till	to	
t.	timme	hour	
tel., tfn	telefon	telephone	
t.ex., t ex	till exempel	e.g.	
tf.	tillförordnad	acting	
t.h.	till höger	to the right	
t.o.m., t o m	till och med	even, up to and including	
tr.	trappa/-or	floor/s	
t.v.	till vänster	to the left	
	tills vidare	for now	
ung.	ungefär	approx.	
uppl.	upplaga	edition	
utg.	utgåva	edition	

utg.	utgivare	publisher
vanl.	vanligen	usually
vard.	vardagar	weekdays
v.	vecka	week
	vers	verse
	vänster	left
	väg	road
	västra	west(ern)
VD	verkställande direktör	managing director
v.g.v.	var god vänd!	PTO
åld.	ålderdomligt	archaic
äv.	även	also
ö.	östra	eastern
	över	over
övers.	översättare	translator

Chapter 14

Orthography

14.1 Small or capital letter?

1 Capital letters are used in Swedish in the same way as in English in the following cases:

(a) At the beginning of a sentence.

(b) After a colon in direct speech: **Herren sade: "Varde ljus."**

(c) In proper names: **Ingvar Andersson, Volvo, Kungsgatan, Malmö, Danmark, "Fadren" av August Strindberg.**

(d) In order to show respect: **Gud, Herren, Hans Majestät Konungen**

2 Small letters are used in Swedish in many cases where English has a capital:

(a) In the names of weekdays, months, seasons and festivals:

måndagen den 6:e juni	Monday the 6th of June
jul, **påsk**, **pingst**, **midsommar**	Christmas, Easter, Whitsun, Midsummer

(b) In nouns and adjectives denoting nationality, language, religion, political affiliation and those deriving from a place name:

Han är tysk men talar svenska.	He is German, but speaks Swedish.
Karl läser en dansk roman.	Karl's reading a Danish novel.
Sven är socialdemokrat.	Sven is a Social Democrat.
Lars är stockholmare.	Lars is a Stockholmer.

217

(c) In titles with names:

Jag har träffat herr Lind, fru Lind, doktor Olsson och ingenjör Ek.

I've met Mr Lind, Mrs Lind, Doctor Olsson and Mr Ek, the engineer.

3 Swedish has a capital only in the first word in names consisting of two or more words (unless any of the subsequent words is itself a proper noun):

	Den helige ande	the Holy Spirit
	Peter den store	Peter the Great
but:	**Svarte Rudolf**	Black Rudolf
	Svenska akademien	the Swedish Academy
	Förenta staterna	the United States
but:	**Republiken Sydafrika**	the Republic of South Africa

This applies also to titles of works of art:

	Röda rummet	The Red Room
	Gamla testamentet	the Old Testament
but:	**Sommaren med Monika**	Summer with Monika

Exceptions: include street names in two or more words (**Södra Vägen, Östra Hamngatan**) and certain other familiar names:

Kungliga Biblioteket	the Royal Library
Sveriges Radio	Swedish Radio

4 Swedish compound nouns usually have a capital letter on the first element if the second element is a proper noun:

	Sydamerika	South America
cf.:	**södra England**	Southern England
	Nordsverige	Northern Sweden
cf.:	**norra Sverige**	Northern Sweden
	Mellaneuropa	Central Europe
	Storstockholm	Greater Stockholm

5 Swedish sometimes has capital letters in correspondence for **Ni, Er** and occasionally for **Du, Dig, Din,** though these are falling out of use. (See 5.2, 5.7.)

6 In Swedish a new line of poetry or song does not automatically begin with a capital letter. In most instances capitals are used in poetry and song in the same way as in text.

 ## Spelling of words ending in *-m, -n*

1 Final **-m** is not doubled even after a short vowel:

dum, hem, rum, program, Glöm det!   Forget it!

Exceptions: damm, lamm

2 Final **-n** is not doubled in many words even after a short vowel:

man, din, vän, in, igen, kan, men, min, mun, män, än, sin, sen (sedan)

Exceptions: grann, sann, tunn, fann (←finna), hann (←hinna), känn (←känna)

3 Between vowels **-m, -n** are always doubled after a short vowel:

hem – hemmet	**rum – rummet**
man – mannen	**vän – vännen**
dum – dumma	**allmän – allmänna**
in – inne	**fram – framme**

4 A word containing **-mm-** or **-nn-** drops one **-m** or **-n** when a consonant is added in an inflected form, e.g. an adjective in the neuter form or a verb adding a weak past tense ending.

ett nummer – numret	**tunn – tunt**
glömma – glömt	**en sommar – somrar**
gammal – gamla	**känna – känt**

Exceptions:
(a) Before the s-genitive: ett lamms svans
(b) Before the s-passive: det känns varmt
(c) Before a suffix: kännbar, tunnhet
(d) In compounds: tunnbröd, dammkorn

Chapter 15

Punctuation

In many cases English and Swedish punctuation is similar. Only the main points and major differences are listed in the paragraphs below.

15.1 The comma

1 The comma is generally used:

(a) Between main clauses in the same sentence, if it is necessary for clarification:

Landslaget vann matchen, och alla gick hem glada.
The national team won the match, and everyone went home happy.

(b) Around any words that are parenthesized or in apposition:

Många små fabriker, såsom Åkerströms, har stängt.
Many small factories, such as Åkerströms, have closed.

Bo Hansson, Malmö FF, var landslagets bästa spelare.
Bo Hansson, Malmö FF, was the best player in the national team.

(c) To mark off exclamations:

Janne, kan du komma ett tag?
Janne, can you come here a moment?

Ja, det kan jag!   Yes, I can!

(d) In decimals:

5,5 procent   5.5 %

Note:
In contrast to English, no comma is used to separate millions, thousands, etc. in expressions such as:

3 000 [tretusen]   3,000 [three thousand]

2 The comma is *not* generally used:

(a) Before **att** clauses, unless both clauses are long:

 Han sa att han var sjuk. He said that he was ill.

(b) Before subordinate clauses where the subordinator is omitted:

 Han sa han skulle komma. He said (that) he would come.

 Bussen han skulle åka med The bus (that) he was going to
 kom aldrig.   come on never arrived.

(c) Around adverbs:

 Detta är emellertid osäkert. This is, however, uncertain.

(d) After introductory or closing phrases in letters:

 Bäste herr Jansson!   Dear Mr Jansson,

 Med vänlig hälsning   With kind regards,

 15.2 The full stop

The full stop ends a sentence which comprises a statement. It is often omitted in common abbreviations: **t ex, t o m**. See also 13.4.

15.3 The colon

The colon is used in the following ways:

1 As in English, before lists, examples, explanations and summaries.

2 Unlike English, before quotations, dialogue or thoughts in direct speech introduced by a verb such as 'said'. In this case the word after the colon has an initial capital letter:

 Han frågade: – Vad gör du här?
 He asked, 'What're you doing here?'

 Jean: I kväll är fröken Julie galen igen; komplett galen!
 Jean: 'Tonight Miss Julie is crazy again, quite crazy!'

3 In some numerical expressions and a few abbreviations (see also 13.4):

50:95   **50 kronor 95 öre**

S:t (= Sankt)   **St (Saint)**

4 Before all kinds of endings added to a figure, a letter, an acronym, etc.:

25:an   the number 25 (bus, tram, etc.)

Gustaf III:s död   the death of Gustaf III

LO:s regler   the rules of LO (the Swedish Trade
                                         Union Confederation)

15.4 The exclamation mark

This is used more widely in Swedish than in English. It is frequently found
after exclamations, greetings, commands, imperatives and warnings:

Mina damer och herrar!   Ladies and gentlemen.

Vad vackert det var här! How beautiful it is here!

Lycka till!   Good luck!

OBS!   N.B.

15.5 The apostrophe

1 The apostrophe is *not* used with the genitive -s, unlike English (see 3.7.1):

pojkens far   the boy's father

pojkarnas far   the boys' father

2 The apostrophe is used to show the omission of letters:

'dag, ropa' han.   G'day, he shouted.

Note:

There is no apostrophe in the following short forms:

dan (← **dagen**), **stan** (← **staden**), **sa** (← **sade**), **ska** (← **skall**), **nån** (← **någon**)

15.6 Direct speech conventions

The most common Swedish convention for indicating direct speech in printed Swedish is the use of a dash ('pratminus') before each speaker's comments. If the words indicating direct speech immediately precede the direct speech, a colon is used instead of the English comma (see 15.3 above):

Polisen frågade: – Vad heter du?
– Martin, kom svaret.
– Och var bor du?
Martin viskade: – Stockholm. Eller rättare sagt, Bromma.

Also used in printing is the guillemet:

»Vad heter du?»

Also used in manuscript is:

"Vad heter du?"

Note that the form of the inverted commas in Swedish ("...") differs from that in English ("...").

15.7 The hyphen

The hyphen is used:

1 In some compound proper nouns:

Karl-Erik, Peterson-Berger, Malmö-Köpenhamntåget

2 In cases where two first elements share a common second element:

sön- och helgdagar	=	**söndagar och helgdagar**
bok- och pappershandel	=	**bokhandel och pappershandel**

3 In compounds with icke-:

icke-rökare	non-smoker
icke-spridningsavtal	non-proliferation treaty

4 In compounds where the first element is an acronym. See also 13.3(4):

LO-kongressen	the Swedish Trades Union Congress	223
T-banan	the Stockholm underground	

5 In compounds where the first element is a number. For compounding see 13.1:

en 50-öring, 1980-talet

6 In certain compounds which would otherwise be too long or complex:

gör-det-själv-kampanjer, öga-för-öga-principen

Chapter 16

Written and spoken Swedish

This section deals briefly with some constructions and word choices generally found only in written or only in spoken Swedish. For a general account of pronunciation, see Chapters 1 and 2; for a few specific peculiarities of pronunciation, see Sections 1.2.10–1.2.11; for some syntax differences between spoken and written Swedish, see 12.8.3(2).

16.1 Words frequently omitted in spoken Swedish

1 Subordinating conjunction **att** after verbs of saying, thinking, perceiving:

Hon sa hon hade läst brevet.	She said she'd read this letter.

2 Relative pronoun **som** as object:

Mannen jag pratade med heter Jansson.	The man I spoke to is called Jansson.
cf. **Mannen** (subject) **som kom heter Johansson.**	The man who came is called Johansson.

3 Verbs of motion after a modal auxiliary:

Jag måste till Lund idag.	I have to go to Lund today.
De ville hem.	They wanted to go home.
Vi ska bort.	We are going away.

4 The pronoun **jag** when in an initial unstressed position:

Hade tänkt vi skulle på bio.	Thought we might go to the cinema.

16.2 **Words and constructions frequently inserted in spoken Swedish**

The following usages are more common in spoken than in written Swedish:

1 Formal subject (see 12.6.1, 12.7.7):

Det satt två gubbar på en bänk.	There were two old men sitting on a bench.
(cf. **Två gubbar satt . . .**	Two old men were sitting . . .)

2 Cleft sentence (see 12.7.8):

Det var han som tog pengarna.	It was him who took the money.
(cf. **Han tog pengarna.**	He took the money.)

3 Duplication (see 12.5):

Han som står därborta, honom känner jag.
Him standing over there, I know him.

Jag har inte varit där, inte.
I haven't been there, I haven't.

4 Supplementary **du** in commands:

Kom hit, du!	Come here! (See 7.5.13)

5 Supplementary **så** and **då**:

(a) After an adverbial as topic:

Förr i tiden, så/då hade man inte TV.
In the old days we didn't have TV.

(b) After a subordinate clause as topic, introduced by **när, om, sedan**:

När han kommer, så kan vi börja.
When he arrives, (then) we can start.

6 The particles **ju, nog, väl, nämligen**

These adverbs are used in speech to alter the sense of a statement subtly by indicating the speaker's/listener's (likely) reaction to it. See 8.4(7).

Words usually found only in written Swedish

Some words and constructions found in written Swedish may sound stilted in informal written or in spoken Swedish. In the table below somewhat less formal alternatives are suggested:

Written/formal	Spoken/less formal
1 Demonstratives **denne, denna, detta, dessa**	**den, det, de** or: **den här, det här, de här**, etc.
Han älskar denna flicka. He loves that girl.	**Han älskar den flickan.** He loves that girl.
2 Possessive **dess**	End article or repetition of noun in **s**-genitive:
Jag tycker om stugan. Dess läge är så vackert. I like the cottage. Its location is so beautiful.	**Jag tycker om stugan. Stugans läge/ Läget är så vackert.** I like the cottage. The (cottage's) location is so beautiful.
3 Relative **vars**	**som . . . som . . .**
De vars namn börjar på S Those whose names begin with S	**De som har namn som börjar på S** Those who have names beginning with S
4 Conjunction **då**	**när**
Då han fick se mig blev han arg. When he saw me he got angry.	**När han fick se mig blev han arg.** When he saw me he got angry.
5 Conjunction **samt**	**och**
Mannen och hustrun samt barnen The man and his wife and children	**Mannen, hustrun och barnen** The man and his wife and children
6 Conjunction **såväl . . . som**	**både . . . och**
Såväl lärda som olärda lyssnade på honom med behållning. Both educated and uneducated benefited from listening to him.	**Både lärda och olärda lyssnade på honom med behållning.** Both educated and uneducated benefited from listening to him.
7 Conjunction **så att**	**så**
Han åt så att han blev sjuk. He ate so that he was sick.	**Han åt så han blev sjuk.** He ate so that he was sick.
8 Conjunction **därför att**	**för att**
Jag säger det inte därför att jag vill klandra. I do not say this because I wish to criticize.	**Jag säger det inte för att jag vill klandra.** I do not say this because I wish to criticize.

9 Adverb **även**   **också/med**

Anders reste sig, och det   **Anders reste sig och det gjorde**
gjorde även Bertil.   **också Bertil/det gjorde Bertil med.**
Anders got up, as did Bertil.   Anders got up, as did Bertil.

10 Conjunction **såsom**   **som, liksom**

De gjorde såsom de hade   **De gjorde som de hade blivit**
blivit befallda.   **befallda.**
They did as they had been told.   They did as they had been told.

Linguistic terms

This list comprises only those terms that may not be familiar to a student of language or those that are not already explained in the text. In some cases these are not directly transferable to English grammar.

ABSTRACT NOUNS refer to nouns expressing unobservable notions, e.g. **svårighet, musik, påstående**, difficulty, music, assertion.

ADJECTIVE PHRASE consists of an adjective or a participle with optional words which modify or limit its meaning, e.g. **Han är** (*ganska*) *dum*, He is (rather) silly.

ADVERB PHRASE consists of an adverb with optional words which modify or limit its meaning, e.g. **Han körde** (*ganska*) *fort*, He drove (quite) fast.

ADVERBIAL (see CLAUSAL ADVERBIAL, OTHER ADVERBIALS)

AFFIX is a prefix added to the beginning, or suffix added to the end, of a word, e.g. **olycklig**, unhappy; **god***het*, goodness.

AGENT is the person or thing carrying out the action. In a passive construction it is realized through an **av** phrase, e.g. **Bilen kördes** *av* *inspektören*, The car was driven by the inspector.

AGREEMENT is a way of showing that two grammatical units have a certain feature in common, e.g. **min***a* **hund***ar*, my dogs (plural); **slott***et* **är stor***t*, the castle is big (neuter).

APPOSITIVE means standing in APPOSITION.

APPOSITION is where two noun phrases describe the same phenomenon, e.g. *Olle, min bror*, **är sjuk**, Olle, my brother, is ill.

ASSIMILATION is the process whereby a sound changes to become more like or identical with another sound, e.g. pronunciation of **min bror** as [mimbrɷ:r] where [n] changes to [m] before [b]. The two sounds may merge completely, as in the case of **-d** in the past tense of the verb **använda** + *-de* → **använde**.

ATTRACTION is a grammatical error often caused by the speaker's losing sight of the true AGREEMENT and becoming distracted by another word, e.g. *Typiskt* **för detta barn är en viss blyghet**, Typical of this child is a certain shyness. This should read **Typisk** to agree with non-neuter (**en**) **blyghet**.

ATTRIBUTIVE is used to describe adjectives that precede the noun and modify it, e.g. **ett** *stort* **hus**, a big house.

CLAUSAL ADVERBIAL denotes an adverb modifying the sense of the clause as a whole, e.g. **Han är** *inte* **dum**, He's not stupid; **De är** *aldrig* **lata**, They are never lazy; **Studenterna är** *förmodligen* **intelligenta**, The students are presumably intelligent.

CLAUSE is a syntactic unit that usually consists of at least a finite verb and a subject (though the subject may be understood, as in most imperative clauses, e.g. **Skjut inte budbäraren!**, Don't shoot the messenger!). There are two major types of clause: main clauses (MC) and subordinate clauses (SC), e.g. **Middagen stod på bordet** (MC), **när jag kom hem** (SC), The dinner was on the table when I got home. (Cf. SENTENCE.)

COLLECTIVE NOUNS are nouns whose singular form denotes a group, e.g. **familj**, family; **boskap**, cattle.

COMMON NOUNS are all nouns that are not PROPER NOUNS, e.g. **en hund**, a dog; **två katter**, two cats.

COMPLEMENTS express a meaning that adds to (or complements) that of the subject or object. They can be either an ADJECTIVE PHRASE or a NOUN PHRASE, e.g. **Olle och Sven är** *intelligenta*. **De är** *studenter*. Olle and Sven are intelligent. They are students.

COMPLEX VERB has two or more parts: **Jag** *har ätit* **sniglar**, I have eaten snails.

COMPOUND VERB is a verb consisting of a STEM and a prefixed PARTICLE, which may be inseparable or separable from the stem, e.g. *betala*, pay, but **köra** *om*/*om*köra, overtake.

CONGRUENCE (= AGREEMENT)

CONJUGATION denotes the way a verb is inflected, its pattern of endings, and also the different groups of verbs with the same endings, e.g. past tenses in: Conj. I **kalla-de**, Conj. IIb **köp-te**, Conj. III **bo-dde**.

COPULAR verbs (or copulas) link the noun or adjective complement to the subject, e.g. **Han** *är* **lycklig**, He is happy; **Eva** *blev* **läkare**, Eva became a doctor; **Sven** *blev* **besviken**, Sven was disappointed.

COPULATIVE means 'linking' (see COPULAR).

CORRELATIVE is the word or phrase that a pronoun replaces or refers to, e.g. **Filmen** is replaced by **som** in **Filmen som vi såg var urfånig**, The film that we saw was really silly.

COUNT NOUN is a noun that describes an individual countable entity and therefore usually possesses a plural form, e.g. **bok – böcker**, book-s; **ägg – ägg**, egg-s; **pojke – pojkar**, boy-s.

DECLENSION denotes the different ways of INFLECTING the noun in the plural, e.g. **flick*or*, pojk*ar*, park*er*, äppl*en*, män, bestsellers** (girls, boys, parks, apples, men, bestsellers). It is also used to describe adjective + noun constructions such as the indefinite declension of the adjective, e.g. **en sådan liten bil**, a little car like that, or the definite declension of the adjective, e.g. **den lilla bilen**, the little car.

DEFINITE refers to a previously mentioned entity, cf. ***Tjuven* har stulit klockan**, The thief has stolen the clock. The INDEFINITE refers to a new entity, e.g. ***En tjuv* har stulit klockan**, A thief has stolen the clock.

DERIVATIVE refers to a word derived from a STEM, usually by the addition of an AFFIX; e.g. **angå**, concern; **begå**, commit and **föregå**, precede, are all derivatives of the verb **gå**, go.

DIRECT OBJECT refers to a person or thing directly affected by the action of a (transitive) verb, e.g. **Pojken slog *bollen/sin syster***, The boy hit the ball/his sister.

DUPLICATION involves the repetition of a subject, object or adverbial, usually in a pronoun or adverb form, e.g. ***Olle*, han är inte dum, *han***, *Lit.*: Olle, he isn't stupid, he isn't.

DURATIVE VERB (or verb of duration) denotes a continued action (e.g. **sova**, sleep), a constant change (e.g. **växa**, grow) or an intermittent action (e.g. **droppa**, drip).

ELLIPSIS involves the omission of a word or word group in the sentence, e.g. **Jag ville röka men jag fick inte** (*röka*), I wanted to smoke but I was not allowed to (smoke).

END WEIGHT is the principle that long, heavy expressions come at the end of the sentence, e.g. **Han åkte sedan *med en gammal lastbil utan strålkastare***, He then travelled in an old truck without lights.

FINITE VERB is a verb showing by its form tense, mood or voice (active/passive) (cf. NON-FINITE VERB).

FORMAL SUBJECT is is an element (**det** in Swedish, 'it' or 'there' in English) inserted to occupy the position before the verb in clauses where the REAL (or GRAMMATICAL) SUBJECT is postponed, e.g. ***Det* (FS) sitter en gubbe (RS) därborta**, There's an old man sitting over there.

FRONTING is moving an element to the beginning of the sentence, cf. **Vi älskar *rödvin***, We love red wine, and ***Rödvin* älskar vi**, Red wine we love.

GENDER can be by sex: **pojken – han**, the boy – he, **tjejen – hon**, the girl – she, or grammatical gender: **ett hus, ett barn; en matta** (a house, a child, a carpet).

GRAMMATICAL SUBJECT (= FORMAL SUBJECT)

HOMOPHONE is a word that is identical in sound to another word, e.g. **komma** = either 'to come' or 'comma'.

IMPERATIVE is the mood of the verb expressing command or warning or direction, e.g. **Kom!**, Come on!; **Rör om!**, Stir.

IMPERSONAL constructions do not involve a person but usually the impersonal pronoun **det**, e.g. **Det snöar**, It's snowing.

IMPLIED SUBJECT is actually an object which functions as subject in a non-finite clause, e.g. **Vi bad** *honom* **skriva en rad**, We asked him to drop us a line.

INDECLINABLE describes a word that does not INFLECT, e.g. the adjectives **bra**, good; **utrikes**, foreign; **öde**, deserted, which take no endings for neuter or plural.

INDEFINITE (cf. DEFINITE)

INDIRECT OBJECT is usually a person or animal benefiting from an action: e.g. **Vi gav** *honom* **pengarna**, We gave him the money.

INFINITIVE PHRASE is a phrase consisting of an infinitive accompanied by optional words which modify it, e.g. **att skriva brev**, to write a letter.

INFLECT means to change form by modifying an ending, e.g. the verb **skriva** (write) inflects **skriv, skriva, skriver, skrev, skrivit, skriven**; the noun **bil, bilen, bilar, bilarna, bilarnas**, the adjective **rolig, roligt, roliga**, etc.

INFLEXIBLE (= INDECLINABLE)

INFLEXION (see INFLECT)

INTERROGATIVE means question, e.g. an interrogative pronoun asks a question: *Vem* **var det?**, Who was that?; *Varför* **kom du hit?**, Why did you come here?

INVERTED word order denotes verb–subject order, e.g. **Idag åker vi**, Today we leave.

MATRIX is that part of a main clause sentence remaining when the subordinate clause is removed, e.g. *Eva lovade* **att hon skulle skriva till oss**, Eva promised that she would write to us.

MORPHEME is the smallest part of a word expressing some meaning: in the word **bilarna**, the cars, there are three morphemes: **bil**, 'car', **ar**, plural morpheme, **na**, definite morpheme.

MUTATED VOWEL is one that changes in different forms of the word, e.g. o → ö in **son – söner**, son – sons; **stor – större**, big – bigger.

NOMINAL means a word or phrase acting as a noun, e.g. **Boken är intressant**, The book is interesting. Some verbs and adjectives can also be used nominally: *Att simma* **är roligt**, To swim is fun; **den** *gamla*, the old woman.

NON-COUNT NOUN is a noun, often denoting an abstract or substance, that does not usually take a plural, e.g. **mjöl**, flour; **bensin**, petrol; **luft**, air; **vatten**, water; **glädje**, joy.

NON-FINITE VERB forms are those forms not showing tense or mood, namely infinitive, supine and participles.

NOUN PHRASE is a noun often accompanied by one or more words before or after the noun which modify it, e.g. **en vacker dikt som jag lärde mig**, a beautiful poem that I learned.

NUMBER is a collective term for singular and (usually marked by an ending) plural, e.g. **en penna**, one/a pen, **två pennor**, two pens.

OTHER ADVERBIALS (or content adverbials or sentence adverbials) are usually an adverb, noun phrase or subordinate clause denoting manner, place, time or condition, e.g. **Han åker** *med tåg* (Manner) *till Stockholm* (Place) *i morgon* (Time) *om han har tid* (Condition), He will travel by train to Stockholm tomorrow if he has time.

PARENTHETICAL means bracketing, e.g. the prepositional expression *för* **10 dagar** *sedan*, ten days *ago*.

PART OF SPEECH means word class, e.g. noun, adjective, verb, conjunction etc.

PARTICLE is a stressed adverb or preposition appearing together with a verb to form a single unit of meaning, as a particle verb, e.g. *om* in **köra om**, overtake; *ned* in **skriva ned**, write down.

PARTITIVE indicates that a part is implied, e.g. **en del av pengarna**, some of the money; **en flaska vin**, a bottle of wine, **ett kilo potatis**, a kilo of potatoes

PEJORATIVE means deprecating as in e.g. **din dumma åsna**, you stupid ass.

PERIPHRASTIC means paraphrasing.

POSTPOSITIONED means coming after another sentence element.

PREDICATE forms the only compulsory part of the clause other than the SUBJECT. The predicate is the verb plus any object, complement or adverbial: **Han** *spelar* (*piano dagligen*), He plays (the piano every day).

PREDICATIVE(LY) indicates that an element is found after the verb.

PREDICATIVE COMPLEMENT is a word or word group (often a NOUN PHRASE or ADJECTIVE PHRASE) which complements, i.e. fills out, the subject, e.g. **Hon är** *hans lärare* **och hon säger att han är** *lat*, She is his teacher and she says that he is lazy.

PREPOSITIONAL PHRASE consists of a preposition plus a prepositional complement (usually a NOUN PHRASE or INFINITIVE PHRASE), e.g. **flickan** *med det långa håret*, the girl with the long hair; **flickan gick** *utan att säga adjö*, the girl left without saying goodbye.

233

PRE-POSITIONED means coming in front of another element.

PRODUCTIVE implies that a word class or method of word formation is still being used to produce new words, e.g. the suffix -vänlig in **sittvänlig**, comfortable to sit in.

PROPER NOUNS are names of specific people, places, occasions or events, books, etc., e.g. **Olle, Stockholm, Krig och fred**.

RAISING is the practice of moving an element from a subordinate clause to the front of the main clause (cf. FRONTING), e.g. *Det* sa Pelle att vi inte skulle göra, Pelle said that we should not do *that*.

REAL SUBJECT is the postponed subject, e.g. **Det är roligt** *att dricka vin*, It's nice to drink wine. (See FORMAL SUBJECT.)

RECIPROCAL or RECIPROCATING indicates a mutual activity in either the pronoun, e.g. **De älskar** *varandra*, They love one another, or in the verb, e.g. **De kysstes länge**, They kissed for a long time.

REFLEXIVE applies to both pronouns and verbs. Reflexive pronouns refer to the subject in the same clause. They have a distinct form in the 3rd person, e.g. **Han har rakat** *sig*, He has shaved (himself). Reflexive verbs incorporate such a pronoun: **De har** *lärt sig* **svenska**, They have learned Swedish.

SEMANTIC denotes the meaning of words.

SENTENCE is a syntactic unit that contains a complete meaning and consists of one or more clauses (cf. CLAUSE). Thus the following three examples are all sentences: **Titta där!**, Look there!; **Hon tar bussen, när det regnar**, She takes the bus when it rains; **Om du tror, att jag kan komma ihåg, vad han sa, när vi besökte honom förra veckan, har du fel**, If you think that I can remember what he said when we visited him last week, you're wrong.

SIMPLE VERB is one that only consists of one word, e.g. *hjälp!*, help!; (han) *sover*, (he) sleeps; (han) *gick*, (he) went.

STATEMENT is a declarative sentence or clause ending with a full stop: **Numera finns det vargar i norra Sverige**, Now there are wolves in Northern Sweden.

STEM is the part of the verb common to all of its forms and to which the inflexional endings are added, e.g. *dansa, dansar, dansade, dansat*.

SUPINE is an indeclinable form of the verb used together with the auxiliary verb **har** to form the perfect tense and **hade** to form the pluperfect tense: **Jag har/hade målat badrummet**, I have/had painted the bathroom.

SYLLABLE consists of a vowel plus one or more consonants, e.g. **ö, dö, rör, röst, in-du-stri-ar-be-ta-re**.

TAG QUESTION comes at the end of a statement and invites a response from the listener. In English it consists of verb + subject (+ negative):

He likes salmon, *doesn't he*? In Swedish **va?** or **eller hur?** usually suffice: **Han gillar lax**, *eller hur?*

TERMINATIVE VERBS denote an action or process implying a state of change or leading to a change or cessation, e.g. **somna**, fall asleep; **låsa**, lock.

TOPIC is the position at the beginning of all main clause STATEMENTS and v-questions. It is usually occupied by the subject, e.g. **Vi/*Studenterna* tycker om öl**, We/The students like beer. But in Swedish, non-subjects, especially ADVERBIAL expressions of time or place, often occupy the topic position, e.g. *I morgon* **spelar jag fotboll**, Tomorrow I'm playing football.

V-QUESTION is a question beginning with a v-word, e.g. **vad, vem, vilken, var** plus **hur** and **när: Vad gör du?** Vad are you saying?

VERB PHRASE consists of a FINITE VERB alone or several finite and NON-FINITE VERBS in a chain, e.g. **Han** *reser*, He is travelling; **Han** *måste kunna springa*, He must be able to run.

VOICED indicates a consonant produced with vibration of the larynx, e.g. **b, d, g, v, m, n, r, l.**

VOICELESS indicates a consonant produced without vibrating the larynx, e.g. **p, t, k, f, s, z.**

Short bibliography

Ahlgren, Jennie, Holmes, Philip and Serin, Gunilla, *Colloquial Swedish*, Routledge, London, 2 ed., 2006.

Andersson, Erik, *Grammatik från grunden*, Hallgren & Fallgren, Uppsala, 2 ed., 1994.

Andersson, Lars-Gunnar, *Vi säger så*, Norstedts ordbok, Stockholm, 2000.

Andersson, Lars-Gunnar and Ringarp, Anna Lena, *Språket, Svenska folkets frågor till radioprogrammet Språket,* Norstedts, Stockholm, 2006.

Bonniers svenska ordbok, Albert Bonniers Förlag, Sverige, 2006.

Elert, Claes Christian, *Ljud och ord i svenskan 2*, Almqvist and Wiksell, Stockholm, 1981.

Holm, Lars and Larsson, Kent, *Svenska meningar*, Studentlitteratur, Lund, 1980.

Holmes, Philip and Hinchliffe, Ian, *Swedish Word Formation. Introduction and Exercises*, Hull, 1995.

Holmes, Philip and Hinchliffe, Ian, *Swedish: A Comprehensive Grammar*, Routledge, London, 2 ed. 2003.

Jörgensen, Nils and Svensson, Jan, *Nusvensk grammatik*, Liber, Malmö, 1986.

Kjellin, Olle, *Svensk prosodi i praktiken*, Studieförlaget, Uppsala, 1978.

Lindberg, Ebba, *Beskrivande svensk grammatik*, AWE Gebers, Stockholm, 2 ed., 1980.

Montan, Per and Rosenqvist, Håkan, *Prepositionsboken*, Skriptor, Stockholm, 1982.

Nationalencyklopediens ordbok, 3 vols, Höganäs, 1995.

Natur och Kulturs stora svenska ordbok, Natur och Kultur, Stockholm, 2006.

Norstedts förkortningsordbok, Norstedts Akademiska Förlag, Stockholm, 2003.

Norstedts svenska ordbok, Norstedts Akademiska Förlag, Stockholm, 2004.

Norstedts Stora Svensk-Engelska Ordbok, Norstedts Ordbok, Stockholm, 2000.

Språkriktighetsboken, Skrifter utgivna av Svenska språknämnden 93, Stockholm, 2005.

Svenska akademiens ordlista över svenska språket, Norstedts, Stockholm, 13 ed., 2006.

Svenska skrivregler, Svenska språknämnden, Stockholm, 2 ed., 2000.

Svenskt språkbruk, Ordbok över konstruktioner och fraser (utarbetad av Svenska språknämnden), Norstedts, Stockholm, 2003.

Thorell, Olof, *Svensk grammatik,* Esselte Studium, Stockholm, 2 ed., 1977.

Thorell, Olof, *Att bilda ord,* Skriptor, Stockholm, 1984.

Ulf Teleman, Hellberg, Steffan and Andersson, Erik, *Svenska Akademiens grammatik,* 4 vols, Stockholm, 1999.

Wellander, Erik, *Riktig svenska,* Norstedts, Stockholm, 3 ed., 1973.

Wessén, Elias, *Vårt svenska språk,* Almqvist and Wiksell, Uppsala, 3 ed., 1970.

Wijk-Andersson, Elsie, *Ny grammatik. Det svenska språkets struktur,* Studieförlaget, Uppsala, 1981.

Åkermalm, Åke, *Modern svenska,* Gleerups, Lund, 3 ed., 1979.

Index

Numbers refer to *paragraphs* and *sub-paragraphs*. Words in ordinary type are linguistic terms. Words in bold are Swedish. Words in italics are English.